The Memoirs of
COUNT APPONYI

THE MACMILLAN COMPANY
NEW YORK · BOSTON · CHICAGO · DALLAS
ATLANTA · SAN FRANCISCO

Count Albert Apponyi

From the portrait by Mr. P. A. de László in the National Gallery of Art, Budapest. A copy (also by Mr. de László) has been presented by the Hungarian Government to the Peace Palace in Geneva

The Memoirs of

COUNT APPONYI

THE MACMILLAN COMPANY

NEW YORK :: MCMXXXV

PRINTED IN THE UNITED STATES OF AMERICA
BY THE POLYGRAPHIC COMPANY OF AMERICA, N.Y.

CONTENTS

CHAP.   *Page*

    PREFACE   ix

    FOREWORD   xiii

   I   EARLY YOUTH   1

  II   ON THE THRESHOLD OF PUBLIC LIFE   36

 III   LISZT AND WAGNER   63

 IV   EGYPT SIXTY YEARS AGO AND TO-DAY   108

  V   PERSONAL IMPRESSIONS OF AMERICA   155

 VI   ROME YESTERDAY AND TO-DAY   225

 VII   HOW PEACE WAS MADE AFTER THE
         GREAT WAR   252

VIII   THE CRISIS IN THE LEAGUE OF NATIONS   288

 IX   ON OLD AGE   302

ILLUSTRATIONS

COUNT ALBERT APPONYI   *frontispiece*

COUNT APPONYI'S FATHER   *facing*   8

COUNT APPONYI'S MOTHER   24

COUNT APPONYI AS A YOUNG MAN   40

COUNT APPONYI TALKING TO ADMIRAL HORTHY
    AND CARDINAL CSERNOCH   120

COUNT LÁSZLÓ SZÉCHÉNYI   168

COUNT APPONYI SPEAKING AT A CONFERENCE
    IN PARIS   264

COUNT APPONYI WITH HIS FAMILY   308

PREFACE

In the year 1931 my husband celebrated his eighty-fifth birthday, which almost coincided with the sixtieth anniversary of his entry into Parliament and with his golden jubilee as member for the constituency of the town Jászberény. Parliament, his constituents, and the whole country fêted him on this triple occasion, a national presentation was made to him and he was commissioned to write his political memoirs for the Hungarian nation. During this task there passed before his mind's eye incidents and impressions that went back to the distant years of his childhood, and these might also interest a wider circle of readers.

At the suggestion of some of his friends my late husband decided to arrange these scattered pages in one volume and to publish them. This book contains a few memories from different periods reaching back over eighty years, as well as outstanding impressions which he gathered on his travels and from his meetings with eminent figures in the realm of politics and art. Most important of all to him was music, which lay nearest his heart; his attitude towards it may be seen from the chapter "Liszt and Wagner." All these memories of the distant past and of recent days have had a varied and manifold influence on the author's maturity of character and clearness of vision, until he became the man we knew: a statesman whose views were based on catholic principles, whose way of thought was philosophical, and whose glowing patriotism did not blind him to the rights, conceptions, and feelings of others.

Historical, philosophical, economic and, of course, political studies always attracted the interest of my husband. It would be true to say that until his dying day Albert Apponyi never ceased to learn. He never failed to grasp new ideas and altered circumstances, and he tried to harmonise them with historical experience, national traditions, and Christian morality. Although my husband was always interested in foreign affairs, it was only in the second phase of his public life that he came into close contact with foreign statesmen, through his co-operation in the foundation of the Inter-Parliamentary Union and his active participation in its meetings. Subsequently, his preoccupation with foreign affairs increased inevitably from year to year, as he was sent to Paris as the representative of Hungary for the peace negotiations, and afterwards to the League of Nations as his country's chief delegate; moreover, he collaborated in the effort of securing international understanding and the recognition of equality of rights for all nations, as well as in the endeavour to construct what we hope will be a better future.

The resolute conscientiousness with which he carried out his duties obliged Albert Apponyi to travel to Geneva in 1933, in spite of the bad weather, his great age, and a slight catarrh which had troubled him almost the whole winter. He was impatient to be on the spot in time for the re-opening of the Disarmament Conference, having set his hopes on its success. Soon after his arrival he succumbed to an insidious form of influenza, which was raging in Geneva at the time; in a few days it brought his life and labours to an end. It was wonderful how sincerely the members of the Conference from all over the world, and still more those from Hungary, mourned his loss. Touching, also, was the love and devotion of his king, Otto of Habsburg, who from Belgium hastened to Geneva for a few hours, so as personally to lay a wreath on the bier of his faithful subject, and to say a prayer before it. At a time of deepest sorrow it is consoling to learn that, even in our selfish age, true devotion and sacrifice for great ends, genuine Christianity and loyalty to king and country, earn the general admiration of our contemporaries.

May there be in the future high-minded patriots who will unite love of their country with the spirit of international fellowship, and who will strive to achieve a just and lasting peace, founded on security, for our sorely-tried world. May God give this wish His blessing, but may nations and individual men also give their good-will and unselfish collaboration in the cause of a happier, peaceful future, for which the author of this book confidently hoped.

COUNTESS ALBERT APPONYI.

Budapest, May, 1933.

FOREWORD

IF it is true that the impressions of early childhood leave an indelible mark on one's character, perhaps those who feel any interest at all in my political life—whether friendly or the reverse—may care to trace back that life to its first origins. To this end, I offer as material the following notes. I have gathered them without premeditation or design, exactly as they occurred to me from the abundance of my memories. For in these things only the unpremeditated is genuine and true. If one writes memoirs at all, one should avoid, as far as human weakness allows, the prevalent shortcoming of autobiographers; I mean their desire to justify or extol themselves; their retrospective arrogance which suggests that their author has been an exception to the errors of his times, and yet the actual centre of all events. This tendency is to be found in the memoirs of the most insignificant men, who present even the reminiscences of their childhood as though they were omens of future greatness. I have realised the absurdity of this naïvely subjective method too often not to make every effort, in my own interest, to avoid it.

THE AUTHOR.

CHAPTER I

EARLY YOUTH

I WAS born on the 29th of May, 1846, in Vienna, where my parents were living at that time. My father, Count György Apponyi, who played an outstanding part in the political life of Hungary, was holding the office of resident Hungarian Chancellor at the Viennese Court. My mother was a daughter of Count Albert Sztáray, an influential member of the Hungarian Conservative party; hence I was born into a political circle. Both families, my father's as well as my mother's, belonged to the oldest Hungarian nobility. The first ancestor of the Apponyis about whom we have documentary evidence was Lord Lieutenant of the county of Pozsony at the end of the twelfth century; he is mentioned as a descendant of one of the hundred and seven families who, according to tradition, took part in the migration from Asia. At that time the family bore the name of Péch. It was only under King Sigismund, the Brandenburgian Emperor of Germany, that they exchanged their family estates at Pozsony for the castle of Apponyi and its adjacent lands, hitherto a Royal possession, lying in the county of Nyitra. They adopted the name of this castle, which still belongs to another branch of the family, and have kept the name down to the present day. Tradition has it that the Sztárays are descendants of a Bavarian knight named Wendelin who had entered the service of King Saint Stephen; in reward he was raised to noble rank and received a grant of land. In ancient documents of Hungarian history the name of my fore-fathers is often mentioned, especially at the time of the religious wars; soon after the Reformation they embraced the Lutheran faith, as indeed did a great part of the Hungarian nobility; and it was only at the beginning of the seventeenth century, thanks to the great Cardinal Páz-mány, that they, with many others, were brought back to the Catholic fold. Up to my father's time none of them played a leading part in public affairs. In my grandfather's generation one branch of the family had entered the diplomatic service. From 1730 to the 70's of the 18th century Count Antal Apponyi and his son Rudolf held with the utmost distinction the posts of Ambassador to Paris and London. From his earliest youth my father took part in the internal politics of our country. He began his career in the county administration, and this completely severed him from the way of thought under Maria Theresa, and to which his grandfather had still belonged; it also rooted him again in the ancestral soil of his mother country.

My earliest recollection of myself and of my first

recorded utterance derives from what my parents told me, not from my own memory. It occurred in the course of the year 1848, when I was about two and a half years old and had just begun to talk; I then produced a sentence of a political complexion which contained a wealth of wisdom I have never since surpassed! In those days my father was Hungarian Court Chancellor in Vienna, and was obliged on one occasion, on account of dangerous rioting, to leave the town with his family in the middle of the night. I was awakened from my sweet slumber and dressed; the interruption of my night's rest made me most indignant. But they said that there was nothing to be done, that we must clear out because of the Revolution. It was on this occasion that I made the memorable pronouncement which was also my first expression of political opinion:— "Silly revolution! One can't even sleep in peace!"—Now I wonder, what does this foretell for the future of the youthful politician? A reactionary in the making, to whom every revolution is an outrage? or do we hear a progressive statesman warning me against too much sleep? I do not undertake to answer this question myself; it is specially difficult as there was a lengthy interruption caused by a completely non-political interval, and therefore the thread of logical development between my first utterance and my subsequent career is hard to disentangle.

The circle in which I was born, grew up, and was privileged to belong to until the early years of my manhood, was the happiest imaginable. My parents were people who possessed uncommon spiritual qualities, both as regards mind and character; and the perfect harmony and intimacy of their married life had not been interrupted for a single moment even by the slightest quarrel.

My mother, alas, died early; she was only in her fiftieth year, and I myself twenty-three. There were only the two of us; my sister Georgina and myself, and I was by five years her junior. Our intimate family circle was completed by the closest relatives of my parents, among whom were a number of very remarkable women. One of these, the widow of Count Antal Apponyi, Austrian Ambassador to Paris in Charles X's and Louis Philippe's time, was a descendant of the Nogarola family, which during the Renaissance had given birth to the famous humanist Isotta Nogarola. Countess Antal Apponyi enjoyed a world-wide reputation for kindness and charm, and it should be said that the source of her charm lay in her warmth of heart. She often came to visit my parents, and inspired us children with a feeling of enthusiastic admiration. The same feelings were aroused in us by my father's sisters, who were intimate friends of my mother. One of these was already at that time the widow of Freiherr von Franckenstein who, like many South Germans of the day, had served in the Austrian army, and in the course of his garrison life in Hungary had plucked this rose. The old Frankish noble family, whose name she now bore, had no reason to complain about this Hungarian grafting on to its family tree. My aunt Leopoldina Franckenstein, widowed early in life, not only provided a first-class education for her three sons—the eldest, George, afterwards became with Windhorst leader of the Centre Party and Vice-President of the German Reichstag—but also managed the considerable family fortune with a firm hand and expert knowledge, so that when her eldest son came of age, she was able to hand it over to him in the best possible condition. Together with my mother, whom I can confidently number among the saints, these ladies determined the general conception of womanhood which was unconsciously developing in my mind; women seemed to me in a certain sense higher beings, worthy of profound respect and yet deserving of deepest affection. Whatever I may have had subsequently to reproach myself with, this first impression and this first unconscious attitude towards women have never been completely effaced, and have remained as a blessing to me.

Above all, the relation in which I stood to my parents was the happiest imaginable. For me they were simply the embodiment of what ought to be, their every pronouncement was an incontestable truth, their every decision stood above all criticism. Looking back, I cannot imagine the parents' task being carried out with more understanding and every fulfilment of parental duty than what I experienced at home. While they never allowed discipline to be relaxed, it was a principle which my parents followed in our education that the children should carry away with them a sunny memory of their childhood, and to this end their efforts were always directed.

The political situation in Hungary in the fifties of last century, and other circumstances of a private nature, obliged us to spend the greater part of those years in different places outside my own country; the winters 1853–54 and 1854–55 were passed at Gries bei Bozen in the South Tyrol. I recall those years with particular pleasure. My mind was in the process of awakening, and my parents took good care that this long sojourn abroad should do no harm to my ardent Hungarian patriotism. There was at that time a very talented Hungarian priest in our house who directed the first steps in my education, and never since have I been so completely convinced that everything Hungarian represents the highest degree of human perfection.

Many years after my father's death, I found among his possessions some letters which I had written to him, during a short absence from Griers, when still hardly able to use a pen. I gather from one of these letters that there was often trouble at meal-times, and that I flatly refused certain dishes; so once I wrote to my father: "When they tell me that a dish is Hungarian, I eat it immediately."—All the same, I made an exception of one particular dish which I thought altogether too

6

nasty, and added that I could not believe it was Hungarian.

On birthdays and namedays we often had little theatrical performances in our house, for which my father wrote the text with extraordinary skill. In these plays other children, from among the circle of friends that my parents had soon made, sometimes participated. As far as space permitted, the audience was recruited from all classes of the population, for my father was on friendly terms with many of the local peasants. The performances were in several languages, as they were supposed to assist our French lessons, which had then begun. One Hungarian play had always to be on the programme; thus the less cultured members of the audience were obliged to listen to two-thirds of the performance in a language they did not understand; this made no difference, however, to the popularity of these entertainments.

My father was a first-rate shot and joyfully took part in all the local competitions. At the shooting range in Griers there was once a gala competition, and one stout Tyrolese peasant after a small glass of Ménes wine gave vent to his delight as follows:—"Oh my! This must be what the Mother of God drinks up in Heaven!"—Afterwards the worthy competitors wanted to accompany their host as far as his home. As my mother was ill that day and had to remain in bed, my father asked his companions to be as quiet as possible when they drew near the house where we lived. They obeyed to the letter, talking only in whispers and walking on tiptoe. Quietly, very quietly, they took leave of each other; then the marksmen fell into line under our windows and at a word of command discharged their rifles in one volley. According to their way of thinking, this noise could not disturb anybody!

We spent the summer months of those two years in Schwarzau, where my parents had taken the same Wurmbrand Castle which later belonged to the Grand-Ducal family of Parma and in which the Queen-Empress Zita grew up. In those days only a very small part of the journey, as far as Bruck on the Mur, could be done by train. Afterwards we travelled by post-chaise and the journey lasted, if I remember rightly, five days. On the first occasion we travelled through the Pustertal. On the second journey my parents wanted us to enjoy a few excursions on the way, and we took the road from Bruck direct to Trieste, visiting the Adelberg Grotto, which left me with an impression that is still vivid to-day. From Trieste we went by boat to Venice, unfortunately at night, so that I could not form any idea of the sea, which afterwards became the object of a passionate love. On the other hand, Venice, the city through whose streets one went by gondola, kept my imagination busy for a long time.

We were delayed in Verona because my sister caught chicken-pox, and we had to wait for it to run its course. At that time Lombardy and Venetia were in Austrian possession; a strong garrison was stationed in Verona; and

Count Apponyi's father, Count George Apponyi

its commandant, Freiherr von Wallmoden, and his wife were acquaintances of my parents. Through them we came into contact with the officers of the Garrison, many of whom took their meals in the Hotel where we were staying. It was now that I first made up my mind as to the choice of a profession. We had previously spent a few days at a watering place where a friendly Capucine often accompanied us children on our walks, gladly taking part in our games and our hunts for wild flowers. We had become very attached to him. Not long afterwards when some Hussar officers with whom we had been playing in the Hotel delle Due Torri at Verona, turned to me—then eight years old,—with the usual question as to what I wanted to be when I grew up, my answer was:—"A Capucine!" One can imagine the amusement caused among young Hussar officers by my unusual choice of a career, for I was a very lively boy, rather inclined to mischief. But my early call to be a monk was not to last long. After a few days spent in Verona, and some meetings with the young officers, I made up my mind to become a Hussar, and at no price whatever would I be anything else. As is well known, nothing was to come of this either.

In those Tyrolese years I developed a fairly strong feeling for nature. I loved the high mountains, and, as I was a remarkably good walker, I could accompany my father on many of his rambles to spots commanding a fine view. I took real pleasure in the play of colour of the

9

mountain scenery, in the soft sunset glow that illumined the "Rosen Garten," that splendid range of the Dolomites, which towers over Bozen. Whilst on the subject of my early experiences, I must speak of the impression made on me by a trip to Jenesien, which lies fairly high above Gries, and is a favourite summer resort of the people of Bozen. Our landlord in Gries, a Dr. Neurater, was Burgermaster of Jenesien, and one day he invited our whole party to luncheon. Our company consisted of the Prelate of the Benedictine Foundation in Gries, one or two members of that Foundation, our family, some relations who were staying with us, a Count Fünfkirchen with his daughter,—a slightly older playmate of my sister's,—and a few other people of distinction. The journey was undertaken by part of the company on mountain ponies, by others on foot, and by some of the ladies, amongst them my mother, in Bath chairs from Ischl; for the first time in my life I was allowed to ride. As we approached Jenesien, where the villagers had organised a very festive reception for the guests of their popular Burgermaster, our company was drawn up in military fashion. First came the horsemen, behind them the pedestrians, and lastly the Bath chairs. I was placed as leader at the head of the horsemen, and I discharged this duty with immense seriousness and real elation. For years afterwards I looked upon this day as the happiest in my life; a little vanity played its part in this feeling of delight, but on the whole it was merely innocent enjoyment and pleasure at being in the company of these people.

The fact that I lived among really good and kind people, and that I saw little or nothing of the reverse side of human society, was fundamental to the development of my childhood and youth. I knew that criminals existed, some of whom were hanged and others imprisoned, but I had no inkling that there were also wicked men at large, that everything which people said to us was not necessarily true, or that there were families who lived otherwise than in mutual love and devotion. This pure atmosphere surrounding the years in which my mind was maturing may well have been responsible for an excess of trustfulness in dealing with men, which led to bitter disillusions. But on the whole, I regard it as a blessing, and the tendency to judge men favourably and to approach them with sympathy, which is a still perceptible consequence of it, I regard as an aid to happiness and to the joy of labour in a public career.

One other gift my home bestowed on me which I must count as the greatest blessing of all. A profound faith in the Catholic teaching reigned in my parents' house, together with practical Christianity, and throughout all the years of my development I did not know the meaning of a divergence between theory and practice. In the private chapel that adorns my present country house there is a drawing of the Chapel which we had during our stay at

Gries; its use had been allowed us because my mother was often in ill health. It was in Gries that I learnt, at seven years old, to assist the priest, and the same altar piece that we had there adorns the chapel of my house to-day. It is no masterpiece, but it is an ineffaceable memory, and a feeling of gratitude is attached to it for the best gift that I have carried with me from my beloved home throughout a long life: an unshaken belief in the Catholic faith.

Our family spent the greater part of the years 1855 and 1856 in Baden bei Wien. Here I started my studies preparatory to the University with a capable Hungarian tutor. My first mental contact with politics also occurred at this time, for my father had been one of the leaders of the Conservatives in Hungary before 1848. He belonged to a wing of the party which was as convinced as the most advanced Liberals that we must cut loose from the relics of feudalism in our constitution, and strike out on modern lines in political as well as social life. The Conservatives wished merely to proceed more cautiously, so that the conflicts which afterwards led to the events of 1848–1849 might be avoided. They were thrust on one side by these events, but remained loyal to the King; during the whole period of absolute rule in Hungary, they endeavoured by all means in their power to bring about a return to constitutional government. The wish to remain in constant touch with those who shared his opinions may well have determined my father to make our permanent home in the neighbourhood of Vienna, where alone something could be achieved.

Many visitors with illustrious names from the period of Hungary's political struggles before 1848 came to our Tusculum at Baden. Most noteworthy was the last Transylvanian Court Chancellor, Baron Samu Jósika, who not only possessed outstanding intellectual gifts, but was also a brilliant Latin scholar—no very uncommon distinction among Hungarian politicians at a time when statesmen could still remember Latin as the official language of legislation and administration. But Jósika also cultivated the Roman classics for their own sake, and would examine me sometimes in a jocular manner.

Count Emil Dessewffy, who, though he had never held office, was one of the chief figures in the Conservative party, also came frequently to our house. Among the younger men of note were Count Antal Széchényi and Baron Sennyei, both destined to play a part in politics at the time of my first entry into public life. All these men showed the greatest kindness to the inquisitive boy I then was, and took no offence when I squatted in the corner of the room during their deliberations with my father and greedily drank in every word that was spoken. In this way I evolved a rough picture of the political situation in my country. About its history I already knew a good deal; and my father would laughingly correct whatever exaggerations there might be in this youthful conception, for I had no secrets from him. However imposing he seemed to me, however ready I was to accept his every judgment as incontestable, there was not the faintest trace of fear in this childish worship.

Beside the curiosity—or can I already call it thirst for knowledge?—with which I followed these political discussions, frequent contact with my father's friends developed another wish in me—I might almost say another longing—namely, to know Latin as well as they did. This was naturally very much to the advantage of my studies. I literally devoured everything connected with Latin, and, as I learnt easily, I had acquired an almost perfect mastery of the language on my entry into the second class. It was no longer a subject I had to learn. During the whole course of my studies I read the Latin classics with much the same ease as books in my mother tongue, wrote essays and later made speeches in Latin without any difficulty, and hardly ever made mistakes. This served me well in after-years, for anyone who has much to do with Hungarian constitutional law and history cannot dispense with a knowledge of Latin, as all old laws and political documents are written in that language.

It is, of course, no Ciceronian Latin that is to be found in these faded documents, but one can nevertheless understand it. In my old age I had the opportunity of passing a test on this head. At the great Saint Emery Festival which took place in Budapest in the year 1930, attended by thousands of foreign guests and countless princes of the Church, it was necessary to welcome these dignitaries at the official opening of the gathering. As all countries of the world were represented, in what language was this to be done without offending any of them! An obvious solution was to speak Latin, the language of the Church, and the task of delivering an address of welcome was entrusted to me. I frankly admit that this caused me some little alarm; as it was, however, I acquitted myself of the unaccustomed task without difficulty.

This is anticipating nearly eighty years. The beginning of my middle-school studies in my boyhood brought with it a big change into my life. My parents decided about this time to send me to a boarding school. I felt perfectly happy at home, and gave no grounds for anxiety, apart from an inclination to outbursts of temper which were sometimes extremely violent. But I did not mix sufficiently with companions of my own age, and my parents rightly insisted that this was essential to the formation of my character. My sister Georgina was the only young person at home besides myself;—we were absolutely devoted to each other, and our affection grew into an inspiring friendship that lasted to the end of her life. It was only disturbed now and again when I became jealous of the greater freedom and the completely different treatment accorded her because she was five years older. Such comradeship was not sufficient from an educational standpoint. Both on this account and especially because of the outbursts of temper I mentioned, my parents resolved to send me to a monastic school. Their choice fell on the newly founded Jesuit College at Kalksburg. At the time there was no educational establishment in Hungary in which they would have had the same confidence. We had come into touch with the Jesuits through a prominent member of the Order, Father Matthäus Hoffmayer, who spent a winter in Gries on account of his health while we were there. He became an intimate friend of the family, and through him my parents came to know and trust the Order. I may add that this trust was completely justified throughout the six years I spent in the Jesuit College, and lives on in me unshaken.

The College in Kalksburg had just been opened for the school year 1856–1857, and it only began with the two lowest classes of the "gymnazium." I was put into the second class in the course of the school year; thus I always belonged to the highest form, as the complete Gymnazium was only developed through our being moved up during the six years of my stay there. The College was wonderfully situated. It consisted originally of a private house of medium size, from which eventually grew, as classes and pupils increased, the present imposing building. The severe and overpowering effect of the new building is softened by the irregularity of the old house, which still exists. It stood, and stands to this day, in the midst of a beautiful park, laid out on the last spur of the range of hills, where the famous cold-water spa Kaltenleutgeben—at one hour's walk from Kalksburg—is also situated. The position of the College is ideal both from the point of view of health and from that of its delightful natural beauty.

The external break with family life, which I felt keenly in spite of the interest that everything new has for youth, was softened by the fact that my parents settled in Kalksburg near the College. As they could not yet occupy our future home in Hungary, it made no difference to them where they lived, and Kalksburg offered the same advantages as Baden bei Wien. They built themselves a charming house with a little garden, where we lived for two more years after I left the College. We were unable to return to Hungary because Eberhard Castle near Pozsony, which my father eventually inherited with the adjacent property, was still held by my grandmother the Dowager Countess Apponyi. My parents were on the best of terms with her, and the old, rather ceremonious lady, a perfect example of the aristocrats of the ancient régime, was very glad if we spent a few weeks with her every year; but she would not hear of another family settling in the Castle, and sharing to some extent the management with her. I could tell many amusing tales about those visits of ours to my grandmother; save for myself the whole band of her descendants, some of whom were already grown up, and even middle-aged, were terrified of her. I actually dared to be a little impertinent to her, but this was just what made me her avowed favourite. Perhaps I may turn for a moment to those days, for the whole atmosphere of Eberhard Castle and the outstanding personality of its mistress make a not uninteresting contribution to a study of the period.

She was born a Zichy, and I believe I have her to thank for my longevity; for this is traditional in her branch of the Zichy family, and she herself was well on in the eighties when she first began to lean back while sitting in an armchair or sofa, complaining bitterly that the occasional desire to do this was a sign of premature old age. Up till then, she always sat with her back as stiff as a poker, and naturally everyone had to do likewise; I was the only one who always lolled about with unconscious impudence. She had been educated in the last years before the French Revolution, a time when French manners prevailed in all the smart circles of Europe. A French Order of Notre Dame had founded a boarding school in Pozsony, in which a large proportion of the aristocracy of Western Hungary, including my grandmother, was educated. She spoke French for preference and, although a Zichy, and therefore a member of one of the oldest Hungarian families, she understood not a word of Hungarian. That was the way of the court aristocracy under Maria Theresa. We can almost be grateful to the Emperor Joseph II for his brutal attack on the Hungarian constitution, as this roused the Hungarian and awakened the aristocracy to a consciousness of their national mission. The whole atmosphere at my grandmother's house was French, and she was delighted when as a little boy of seven I could speak French with her for the first time. The prelude to this good impression was, however, of a most peculiar kind, typical, too, of my father, who all his life possessed a great sense of humour, and was occasionally responsible for strange situations! On our way to Eberhard for the first time since I spoke fairly good French, we were all hoping to bring my progress to the knowledge of my grandmother in a suitable way. In the train between Vienna and Pozsony my father said to me in his usual joking manner:—"When grandmother asks you: 'Parlez-vous français?' you must answer: 'Spaghetti in the coffee!'" I listened with imperturbable seriousness, even when my mother said in a slightly reproving tone:—"But, Georges, don't teach the boy such things, he might really say it."—We arrived in Eberhard, where my aunts and other relations were also gathered, so that a fairly numerous company assembled for the excellent, but always cere-monious, dinner party. Everyone was looking with bated breath at the mistress of the house, sitting bolt upright, as they waited anxiously to see what subject she would open, what lead she would give to the conversation at table. Thereupon she turned to me with a gracious smile, and said:—"Eh bien, mon cher Albert, j'entends avec plaisir que vous parlez déjà le français"—upon which I yelled at the top of my voice:—"Spaghetti in the coffee." Picture the great crowd of relations assembled in a ceremonial mood who witnessed such an indescribable piece of bad manners at the table of the stateliest hostess imaginable! Horror was universal, and all grew silent. Yet, strangely enough, my grandmother did not take it at all amiss, but was the first to give the signal for a hilarity that soon became general, mingled with the relief that everyone feels when a great danger has been unexpectedly avoided. After nearly eighty years, I still have this scene before me as if it had happened yesterday, and I confess that I do not recall it exactly with a sense of shame, but have to laugh even now when I remember all the circumstances of the event.

I was very fond of these visits to Eberhard; though I was the only one there who found hardly any amusement, except for a little push-cart and a rubber ball which were always put out for me as a sign of the warm welcome which the house offered to a little boy, and with which I romped around in the beautiful park of the Castle.

"Ma chère solitude d'Eberhard"—I used to say in a romantic vein not quite appropriate to my years; unconsciously, the character and privacy of my surroundings, so harmonious in their way, awoke a certain artistic pleasure in me. The fact is that I enjoyed these visits, even though I was not sorry to go back to Kalksburg.

I cherish a warm and thankful memory of the six years spent there on account of the care and love given to me. Among the many Fathers with whom I came in contact there were naturally men of varying capacities, some more congenial, some less, some better suited to their work than others. But I never met one who was not to be respected as a man and as a priest, and for some of them I could only feel the deepest admiration. There were three in particular who had a profound influence on my development. The first was Father Franz Xavier Hattler, who taught religion in the higher classes, and those scraps of philosophy which were assembled according to the curriculum of the time under the general name of "Introduction to Philosophy." His lectures about religion showed profound philosophical understanding, and were illuminated and inspired by profound piety. His personality was rendered even more impressive because, although scarcely fifty-three, he suffered from a chronic affection of the heart which might have ended his life at any moment. As a matter of fact, he lived on into the seventies. Out of school he was the gayest of men, although he was aware that he walked continually in the shadow of death. This one forgot completely in his company, and it was always a treat for us young people if he took part, as far as his physical strength allowed him, in our conversations and walks. All in all, he was a living sermon on the text that the most extreme asceticism can be united with the simple fulfilment of duty, with unaffected good humour, and with kindness of heart. He inspired me with a liking for philosophical studies which has remained with me throughout my life, to the great advantage of my political career, in that it has stimulated me to obtain a more thorough grasp of the problems with which I have had to deal.

After Father Hattler, Father Spinell, professor of classical philology in the higher forms, had the most lasting influence on me—I might say on us all. I have known greater scholars, but no teacher who was to be compared with him. He simply did not allow anyone to be backward in his subjects: when he discovered that someone was behind, he worked with him privately until the boy got into the first rank again. He organised an "Academy" out of the best pupils in the class, in which they read and studied well-nigh twice as much as was prescribed. For me, perhaps the most amusing of his methods was that which he adopted in oral translation, when he insisted that the translation should be spoken in well-rounded sentences; I am certain that nothing has helped so much to loosen my tongue, and to acquire facility of expression, even in impromptu speeches, as the necessity imposed on me during those years of finding the correct form of words for a given thought. Father Spinell's weakness was a certain nervousness which did not allow him to keep his hands till; he was everlastingly locking and unlocking the drawer of his lecturing desk, which gave us the opportunity for a little practical joke for which I was responsible,—and which I am still glad to remember. I fixed a musical box into the drawer, which could be made to play by pulling a string; after taking the key away, I left this string hanging out of the keyhole. Of course, Father Spinell reached for the absent key of the drawer as soon as he had begun to lecture, and had to content himself, after a little delay, with pulling the string. Then, to everybody's amusement, the music started to tinkle! It would be a mistake to suppose that the good Father was angry about it, or thought of punishments. With the instinct of the born educationalist he was the first to join heartily in our merriment, and even to praise the good joke. Of this man also I cherish a thankful memory.

The third personality of whom I wish to speak was very well known in Vienna at that time; he was the famous preacher, Father Georg Patisz, head of the Order in Austria. For the understanding of what follows, I must explain that I was the spokesman and Public Orator of the College; on all occasions when a speech had to be made in the name of the boys, I was expected to discourse in German, Latin or Greek. At one of the prize-givings, I had prepared myself most conscientiously for this task, as the young orator was of course expected to compose his speech himself. Father Patisz had come to inspect the

College, and when he was told that I had to deliver a speech in the course of the next few days, he wanted to discuss the matter with me. To this end we went for a walk in the park, and the conversation turned on general principles of rhetoric. Our class had just begun the study of Demosthenes, whom I found easy as far as language was concerned, but otherwise he disappointed me. I told Father Patisz quite openly about my feeling of disappointment concerning the great Greek orator; in comparison with Cicero, whose elaborate periods filled me with enthusiasm, I thought him cold, dry and unadorned, and I was unable to understand why he passed for so great a speaker. This led to an extremely interesting discussion, during which the famous preacher said to me:—"If you adopt a career in which you have to speak in public, do not choose Cicero as your master, for his style of oratory is unbearable to modern taste. Choose Demosthenes, in whom what seems austerity to you, is really his compact, logical power of construction. This alone can make an impression on a present-day audience."—I remembered his advice and gradually came to understand Demosthenes, so that I may well say this conversation has had a lasting influence on my development as an orator.

From these details one can form a general idea of the spirit and method prevalent in the management of the school. There was nothing stereotyped or conventional about it, loving care being given as far as possible to every

Count Apponyi's mother, daughter of Count
Albert Sztáray

individual's needs. The work of education was regarded as a lofty calling, not as a business undertaking, or a mere bureaucratic task to be discharged. There was no trace of what opponents of the system have secretly called "Jesuitism," nor could any be detected in the lives of those men who have gone from Kalksburg College into different departments of public life, and who in some cases have become outstanding figures.

Not only the teachers, but also my schoolfellows, helped largely in my education, without, of course, any knowledge or desire on their part. They completely cured me of my fits of rage, so that they never appeared again during the rest of my life. Once more, my parents' foresight proved right, for in their view the best thing for my education was to work in a class, and live at a school together with boys of my own age. The boy who shows signs of bad temper will get no peace from his schoolfellows. Whoever offers a good target for gibes by flying into a temper will be teased mercilessly. This is what happened to me. The principal subject about which I was ragged was the fact, which soon became known, that I had been born in Vienna.—"You aren't a Hungarian, you are a Viennese!"—they shouted at me on the slightest provocation, and this never failed in its effect, to the great delight of my tormentors. These and other jokes provoked me to such an extent that I not only flew at the aggressor with my fists, but would run, if he proved too strong for me, up the three flights of stairs in the school building, and, once in the attic, would relieve my feelings by rolling on the floor and screaming. For nearly a year I was exposed to these attacks on the part of my schoolfellows, among whom I was otherwise popular. I cannot be sure about the date when I seriously turned this subject over in my mind, or, how this actually came about, but as a result of it I said to myself:—"If you did not give the other boys the pleasure of annoying you—which must make you look a fool, anyway--they would soon stop ragging you."—I made the obvious decision and carried it out, by a mental struggle which I can only compare to the cure of a morphia maniac; but I *did* carry it out, and with complete success.

Once I was in the upper forms, the mischief had been overcome, never to reassert itself. I do not think that anyone has seen me in a violent temper within living memory.

Generally speaking, the boys at Kalksburg only came to know intimately the members of one school division, that is to say, of their own form. My form, which was always the senior on account of the fact that lower classes were a later addition, contained on an average between twenty and twenty-five boys, but only eighteen of us sat for the final examination. There were some very clever young fellows among them, and on the whole one could describe the prevailing spirit as exemplary. I was on good terms with all of them, but I only formed real friendship with two, a Count Deym and a certain Johann Schreiber; they were also my rivals for the first prizes. Soon it became a single contest between Clemens Deym and myself; I was his superior in the classical side, he mine in the scientific, especially in mathematics, for which he had an outstanding gift, whereas mine was very limited. The victory swayed between us from year to year, without affecting the warmth of our friendship. I remember how one day in school we were reading a Latin author who spoke of the rivalry of the two orators, Cicero and Hortensius, adding that their struggle to obtain the palm of glory never interfered with the friendship existing between these two heroes of oratory. Deym and I looked up instinctively at the same moment, and we winked at each other, for the passage seemed so appropriate to our relationship. I mention this detail because relationships of that kind between ambitious young men are among the best things which the human spirit can unfold, and which a school can foster. In the interests of truth I must confess that after I had made desperate efforts in mathematics, victory smiled on me. Deym and Schreiber left the school before the close of the six years I spent there; they both entered the priesthood, but died too early to develop completely their abilities in that field. Apart from them I made no friendships with any of my schoolfellows that lasted into later life, though I can only repeat that I was on good terms with them all. I occasionally discussed intellectual questions with a schoolfellow who later took part in Austrian politics, Baron Joseph Dipauli, afterwards Austrian Minister of Commerce. After Kalksburg, he studied at a school in Innsbruck, where he acquired an exceptional knowledge of German literature. This induced me to tell him certain things about Hungarian literature, which seemed likely to display the culture of my nation in a favourable light. For this purpose I even translated a tragedy by Vörösmarty into German iambics, and scored a considerable success with his verses, whose beauty was not entirely lost in my amateurish translation.

I think that these details throw a not unfavourable light on the inner life of the school. Its atmosphere offered much more intellectual stimulus than is usually found at this stage of education, and from the moral point of view no serious objection could be raised against it. Of course there were wild jokes and outbursts of boisterous spirits, as there must always be among young people; but these were mostly of a harmless kind, and whenever a trace of corruption was detected, it was mercilessly and without delay banished from the school. I can truthfully say that I left with the same purity of mind I had brought from my home, strengthened in my faith and with my feet on the right path, and this was the case with an overwhelming majority of the boys.

I must make special mention of the Hungarian circle in Kalksburg. As at the time no similar institution existed in

Hungary, my compatriots were fairly numerous; out of the ninety boys in the College when I took my final examination, twenty to twenty-five must have been Hungarians. There was always a Hungarian Father on the staff, and twice a week a class of Hungarian language and literature was prescribed for the Hungarian pupils. Besides this, so as to have more opportunity of studying our mother tongue, we were often, during the summer months, taken for walks by the Hungarian Father. In the school theatre, which was continually being technically improved, a Hungarian play was produced every year. This had to be so selected from the plays available for our use that every Hungarian boy should have a part, however small. The performances took place before an audience in which nobody understood anything, excepting parents and relations of the Hungarian boys,—if such happened to be in Kalksburg. This, however, did not affect their popularity. For schoolboys it is enough if anything is a "lark." One such performance was the occasion of a little incident which illustrates the spirit of the Hungarians then at Kalksburg. At the time when it happened the theatre was not completed, and the Hungarian performance took place in the refectory. One of the iron pillars of this room divided the stage into two. It had to be turned to some use, and this we found by hanging the Hungarian coat of arms on it, which was very appropriate to the text of our patriotic play. When the stage was cleared away, and the refectory once more served its normal purpose, on the first day the Hungarian coat of arms was left hanging on the pillar. As we left the room after our midday meal, it seemed to one of us that a number of the boys had not behaved respectfully towards the Hungarian coat of arms. In a twinkling, all the Hungarian boys had gathered round the holy symbol to protect it against possible insult— although no one had any such intention. We were full of suspicion, for rumours had reached us about the constitutional struggles which just then, in the Schmerling era, were becoming acute. The Hungarian group waited in front of the column that bore their coat of arms till all the other boys had left the room, and then began to discuss what should be done. It was unanimously agreed, that the holy symbol could not be left in a place where it might not always receive due respect. We took it down with the greatest care, and bore it in procession to the Hungarian Father's room, where we formally surrendered it to his safe keeping.

Such was the Hungarian feeling of my compatriots in Kalksburg. We did not confine ourselves to mere demonstrations, but in every way endeavoured to get time for Hungarian studies. I remember how I sought, and obtained, permission during the summer term before my final examination, to get up an hour earlier, so that I might devote this time to Hungarian literature. I have already described how eagerly I championed that literature among my more gifted schoolfellows, and I am sure that no Hungarian boy lost any of his patriotism by being in Kalksburg. It was one of the educational principles governing the school to encourage the free development of individuality in everything to which no moral objection could be taken. The Fathers had no wish to apply their spiritual teaching as a strait-jacket on the mind, but rather to implant it in such a way that it could be assimilated and absorbed naturally. So it was with religion, and with all branches of knowledge of a distinct ethical character.

Six years had gone by in this atmosphere, interrupted once each year by the long vacation. I was not allowed to go home for Christmas, although my parents lived at a few steps' distance from the College, for no one was permitted to receive favoured treatment. What a glorious time were the holidays spent at home, with excursions and all sorts of entertainments! In my case, when I had reached the upper forms, these vacations always meant fresh contact with political events; I took passionate interest in them, and followed unquestioningly my father's leadership. May I merely mention the years 1861, 1862, and 1863? Whoever recalls the history of those years of constitutional struggle in the Austro-Hungarian Monarchy, and knows something of my subsequent political career, can imagine how eagerly my young heart was beating at that time. Here I must again observe that during those years in Kalksburg serious disagreements about politics were unknown, in spite of the fact that ardent young Hungarians were brought up with an Austrian majority; nor was there any attempt to crush the opinions which were more and more deliberately expressed among the boys as they matured. In 1863 the Matriculation was the chief concern of our thoughts. It hung all the more threateningly over us as at the time Kalksburg was not recognised publicly, and we were obliged to sit for the examination at another school, for which purpose the Theresa College was chosen. It is no small thing to have to pass an examination before professors whom one sees for the first time, and especially the Matriculation, which I sincerely regard as a first-class torture to be condemned on principle. It had to be done, however, and in the hot July of 1863, we travelled daily to the Theresa College in Vienna by carriage, so as to sit for the written examination. Then came the day of our last ordeal: the "oral."

Even now when I drive into the city from the East or the South station as I often do, and when my taxi, which has supplanted the old-fashioned cab, makes its way through the Favoriten Strasse, where the Theresa College stands, I recall the nervous excitement with which I entered that door for the examination in 1863. We were treated in a most considerate way, and the professors who examined us were not only fair, but even showed a certain appreciation of the special difficulty of our lot as complete strangers. I remember the essay which was set us in German during the written examination. We had to write a paper on the famous lines of Goethe: "It is through restraint that the master shows himself, and law alone can give us freedom" —a rather difficult proposition for boys who had only just finished their schooling. This seemed also to strike the supervisor, who felt obliged to give us a few helpful comments.—"D'you see, my young friends,"—he said,— "if you all rushed about wildly in this room, you would always be running into one another and no one would be able to move with real freedom; but if a square space were set aside for the exclusive use of each of you, that is to say, if a law were made for this room and its inmates, you would at least be able to move freely within the limits of the square allotted to you."—We all took up this thought in our essays; what other points we made I can no longer remember.

The final result was that from among the eighteen boys of the eighth class at Kalksburg who took the examination with me, only one failed; in other words, he alone was made to sit for an alternative examination. This boy had only come to Kalksburg the previous year, as a great exception to the usual wise rule by which they never took boys who were half grown up. We were of course very angry that this newcomer should have robbed our class of the honour of leaving the examination battle-field with our flag proudly·flying, but even so the result was a brilliant one in the circumstances. As it happens, the one who failed was neither an incompetent nor a lazy boy, proving how far the Matriculation amounts to a game of chance. I was the only one who had the good fortune to get an honourable mention.

And herewith the doors closed on Kalksburg, on my childhood and early youth; their influence on my subsequent life and experience is clearer to me now, as I stand so very near to another portal, than it ever was before. Those first years were not only significant on account of the deliberate education which was given me so wisely and kindly, and which I recall with undying gratitude. They were important, besides, because of the incidental, and partly unconscious ties which they established between me and earlier generations. Through my father and mother and their circle, I was in closest touch with the great pre-1848 generation, and my first ventures in public life were made under the guidance of surviving leaders from that generation, or of their immediate successors. My contact with my grandmother and some of her contemporaries, whom I have only mentioned in a humorous spirit, took me still further back, and gave me an image of a period as remote as Maria Theresa's reign; which, though unappreciated then, crystallised ever more clearly in my recollection. If I add the sixty years of my political activity to these long memories, I think I can claim a certain freedom from the merely transitory events of national life, which change from generation to generation, and a contact with those more lasting things which are destined to survive them.

I stood now on the threshold of a new era, namely University life. But before going I decided to devote a year exclusively to philosophical studies. My parents had no part in this decision except to give their consent. It was a symbol of the tastes which my education had given me.

CHAPTER II

ON THE THRESHOLD OF PUBLIC LIFE

THE University studies which I pursued in Vienna from 1864 to 1866, and in Budapest from 1866 to 1868, did not influence my development in any notable way, although I listened to some famous professors. What I may call my political début, which brought me into touch at the same time with the great figures of Hungarian public life who did not belong to my father's intimate circle, occurred at the beginning of the year 1867. The *Ausgleich** had already been arranged, and only needed to be drawn up in legal form; people everywhere felt cheerful and confident, as a result of what one may call the *"Ausgleich* mood." At the time a deputation of prominent Dalmatian intellectuals had come to Budapest in the hope of establishing direct contact with Hungary, proposing in this way to escape Croatian influence—a very significant illustration of the stage which those countries had then attained in their development. The Italian element was uppermost in the Dalmatian ruling class; all connection with Croatia was looked upon with loathing, and they were endeavouring

* The *Ausgleich* by which the constitution of the Austro-Hungarian Empire was settled.

to enter into more intimate relations with Hungary. This attempt took the form of a great Dalmatian financial enterprise for the advancement of certain cultural and economic interests. At its head stood the political leader of Dalmatia, Bajamonti, who was widely known as the Dalmatian, Ferencz Deák. The deputation had instructions to reach an understanding with the leading personalities in Hungary, and to secure Hungary's direct participation in their scheme. Ferencz Deák and his followers thought it worth while to summon the leaders of all political parties to a conference, before which the Dalmatian emissaries should unfold their plans. My father, of course, took part in this council. However, when the meeting was opened and the Dalmatians were shown in, it was found that these knew no language but Italian, which none of the Hungarians understood. Imagine the scene! They discussed every means of overcoming the difficulty, until at last my father said that he had a son, who was still only a law student, but who had a good knowledge of Italian; if the gentlemen thought it fitting for so serious an occasion, he would send for him. The proposal was gladly accepted, and a quarter of an hour later, though I was scarcely twenty, I stepped into the conference hall to help the great ones of the country out of their dilemma. It can be imagined how important I felt; I have since had many difficult missions to perform, where more important matters were at stake, and where I was facing mightier personalities, but I have never again known the elation of those days. It was so powerful that it banished all sense of embarrassment. I must have managed fairly well, for at the close of the negotiations the illustrious delegates honoured me with friendly remarks, which broke the ice for all time between me and the leading personalities of the country. The Dalmatian affair itself came to nothing.

During my last University years, 1867 and 1868, I had many more opportunities of mixing freely with these great men. I used to go riding in the early morning, and on one occasion I met the Prime Minister, Count Gyula Andrássy, enjoying the same pastime. He invited me to ride with him and used the opportunity to inform himself about the prevailing attitude of youth towards the *Ausgleich*. A powerful movement had asserted itself under constitutional-radical inspiration which refused to tolerate the idea of a common cause with Austria, and naturally it had many adherents in the ranks of youth. The majority of my fellow-students, with the ardour and freshness of youthful conviction, supported the leadership of Ferencz Deák, cheering Francis Joseph's coronation with an enthusiasm which drowned all captious criticism. I was able to reassure my illustrious riding companion that his supporters predominated in the ranks of youth, and that there were a number of young men, myself among them, who were deliberately working to preserve and strengthen this attitude among their contemporaries.

Andrássy was very interested by this information; he gave me much useful advice, which I was to repeat to my fellow-students, and many intimate disclosures concerning the psychological basis of the *Ausgleich*, which he alone fully grasped. More important for the future were the lessons and the benefit which I personally derived from his conversation. Andrássy was not only a statesman of genius, but a man gifted with incomparable charm. Even his bitterest opponents could not withstand this charm, as I was to experience afterwards when I unfortunately became one of their number. He was indeed what Ferencz Deák was in the habit of calling him: the man sent by Providence for the *Ausgleich*. This *Ausgleich* problem was not merely of a legal or political nature, but one of century-old antagonisms between a nation and a dynasty, and between nations economically interdependent, yet without any mutual understanding of each other's outlook. It could not therefore be solved completely by legal paragraphs and political agreements. Such technical work had to be completed by a careful and wise adjustment of these antagonisms, by social skill and friendliness; in short, by an approach which could not be governed by hard-and-fast rules, but rather by inborn tact. In this Andrássy was a past-master; his influence was responsible for the constitutional contact between Court and Country in the first two years of the *Ausgleich*. He succeeded in making plain the common interests of Hungary and the dynasty just at a moment when he had to struggle against the remnants of Pan-Austrian prejudice. In short, he was the necessary complement of Ferencz Deák, and without the association of these two men the *Ausgleich* would hardly have been possible. Years afterwards Francis Joseph used to say: "We three made the *Ausgleich:* Deák, Andrássy and I,"—and he lamented the fact that he was the only survivor. When European complications made it necessary for Andrássy to exchange the office of Hungarian Prime Minister for that of Austro-Hungarian Foreign Minister, Ferencz Deák, who had only yielded to this necessity after long opposition, cried out: "Andrássy, you have only one fault. We cannot make a duplicate of you." Indeed, it proved impossible to find even a remotely adequate substitute for Andrássy's skill in the psychological handling of the *Ausgleich*. This was perhaps the reason for the unfortunate turn which events subsequently took.

In the course of time, as a result of my failure to understand his foreign policy, I became a keen opponent of Andrássy. This resulted in a certain tension, which lasted for the remainder of his life, and robbed me of a friendship that might otherwise have grown up between us in the years of maturity. I took up the thread again with his son Gyula, also a very gifted statesman, but for the attacks which I had delivered on him in error, though always in good faith, I could

Count Apponyi as a young man

only make amends to the dead man's memory.

I was in constant touch with yet another great figure of those days, Ferencz Deák, who was one of the most eminent survivors of the pre-1848 generation. So also was Baron József Eötvös, then Minister of Education and Culture, whose name is known to every European. He had the good fortune to be surrounded by an unusually congenial family; his wife, Agnes Rosty, was fully competent to grasp his great intellectual significance. She was also a good pianist, and later on, in her widowhood, joined the musical circle about Franz Liszt. Eötvös's son, Lóránt, needs only to be named to the cultured reader; he belongs to the great figures of modern scientific research. My own connection with this circle was formed thanks to the charming daughters of the house, Ilona, who became a Návay by marriage, and Jolán, afterwards Baroness Inkey, two young ladies who united superior qualities of mind and character with extreme kindness, vivacity, and every sort of social talent. They were also excellent dancers, and I was one of their partners. The third daughter, Mária, had hardly entered the "flapper" stage; she afterwards became well known to the Viennese as the wife of the famous Austrian Finance Minister Plener. The mother of these girls invited me, with a few other congenial young people, to visit them in summer at their villa on the Svábhegy, where Eötvös and his family always spent a few months, and from which has grown the monumental sanatorium that crowns the Svábhegy to-day. At that time it was only an unassuming country house, suited to the humble means of this great man. There was no funicular railway, and not even a proper road leading up to it, but only steep, uneven tracks which made bad going for the horses. However, the atmosphere one found there made it worth while to overcome these obstacles. During the summer months, I was a frequent guest at the Villa Eötvös, and my visits often gave me a chance to enter into grave discussions with the master of the house. It was characteristic of him that he did not think it beneath his dignity to talk seriously with young men of my age,—on the contrary, he took pleasure in imparting to them from the treasure-house of his wisdom as much as they were able to grasp. I remember especially our conversations about the social question. Social science was then quite in its infancy, and the teachings of a so-called "Political Economy" held the field in theory and practice. Grave doubts as to this system had already arisen in my mind; I had the feeling that commodities were taking first place at the expense of human beings. Eötvös, who was otherwise a Liberal of the purest dye, though free from the errors of Liberalism in Church and educational matters, kept an open mind about the difficulties of which I spoke to him. As a means of solving them, he referred to the power of association, a prediction that has come true to a degree

42

far surpassing even his foresight. The Liberalism of
Eötvös was free from anti-clerical bias, while in many
countries, and in a greater part of the press, antagonism
towards the Christian—more particularly the Catholic—
faith was the very essence of Liberalism. I experienced
this for myself. In Liberal circles, despite my eventual
support of the principle of equal rights for all, I was never
accepted as a member because I went to Mass. So it was
again in the reactionary period after the Communism; I
was held to be no Christian because I refused to take part
in the persecution of Jews. Eötvös stood honourably and
consistently by the principle of freedom of conscience. He
laboured to maintain good relationships between the
Churches and the State, on the basis of equal rights, which
is the only possible way in a country whose citizens belong
to different confessions. His monumental Elementary
School Act was in accordance with this aim, a measure
whose chief provisions are still in force, and which no one
seriously proposes to alter. The principle on which this
Act is founded is that of liberty in teaching and study.
By placing the State, County and Church schools on an
equal footing under suitable government control, it saved
Hungary from the trials of a *Kulturkampf*, and, moreover,
the application of its main principle to all grades of
teaching made possible the collaboration of every cultural
force in the service of civilisation. Eötvös himself was
very religious, and he always kept up friendly relations

43

with foreign statesmen interested in cultural matters. This was especially the case with the famous leader of the so-called "Liberal Catholics" in France, Count Montalembert, whom we shall meet again in these memoirs. Of Eötvös one can say in truth that no step he took was other than a blessing for his country.

I thus had the unusual good fortune to come into contact with great men while still very young, deriving encouragement and instruction from them. Everything I have here related took place in the course of my last two University years, which came to an end in the autumn of 1868.

I now reached a decision resembling the one taken after my matriculation, by which I devoted a year exclusively to philosophy before entering upon my University studies. As had been the case then, I felt once more the need, after completing my University course, to deepen and perfect what I had learnt there before going further, that is to say, before choosing a career. Accordingly at the end of the last term I only took the so-called law examination, putting off indefinitely, as one was then allowed to do, the second examination in political science. My intention was to devote the two years which separated me from my majority to a study of politics and especially of economics according to my own plan; and also I wished to travel. I felt confident that I could direct these supplementary studies myself. My parents approved of this scheme, which was all the easier to carry out as they had taken up their residence at Eberhard, near Pozsony, in the year 1867, after my grandmother's death. Here was an absolutely ideal spot where I could study completely undisturbed in the most delightful surroundings, and at the same time a convenient starting-point for travel in any direction. As a matter of fact the work and the recreation of those years became a determining factor in my spiritual development.

Very soon, in the spring of 1869, there occurred an interesting episode in my life. For private reasons I had to spend a few weeks in Paris, and I chose to be there during the elections which led to the fall of the imperial autocracy and to the experiment of the "Empire libéral" under the Ministry of Ollivier. Nobody knew then that this was going to happen. It was universally known, however, that there was great excitement in France, and that an important change was likely. I wanted to see this for myself, and the way stood open to me through my father's connection with Count Montalembert, whom I mentioned in connection with Eötvös. Montalembert was also acquainted with other members of my family whom he had met in Rome, but with my father, of whom he had a very high opinion, he had formed a real friendship during his stay in Hungary. Our country and Hungarian affairs had an extraordinary interest for him. He had begun to study them on account of his wonderful work on Saint Elisabeth. I was received by this great man, who was unfortunately very sick, with fatherly affection, and he placed all his social ties at my disposal, so that I might have a chance to see everything that interested me. I could invite myself at any time to take a meal with his family, which consisted of his very clever wife, formerly a Mérode, and his second daughter Madeleine, afterwards Countess Grünne. The elder daughter, Cathérine, had entered the Order of the Sacré-Cœur. From his sick bed, to which he was bound without hope of a cure, owing to the state of medical and surgical knowledge then obtaining, he carried on an enormous correspondence with outstanding men in all lands, kept in touch with leading personalities and with the high clergy of his own country, and was accessible to even the youngest who sought instruction at his hands and had any claim whatever to it. I can hardly say what these three weeks of almost daily contact with this great man meant to me. He honoured me with serious talks, not only about the impressions which I was gathering in Paris, but about great questions of Church policy. Yet even Montalembert, who had been for a generation, both as an orator and as a writer in science, literature, and politics, the consistent and successful champion of Catholic interests, was to experience an attack on his orthodoxy, and to be decried as a heretic, by another school of Catholic politicians, whose chief spokesman was the brilliant writer and journalist, Louis Veuillot. This unfortunate feud, of which every trace vanished many years ago, in those days held the Catholic world in suspense, and was naturally an element of weakness for the cause of the Church. I stood whole-heartedly by Montalembert and his supporters, who included, or had included, some of the greatest contemporary figures in the Church. One of these was the famous Dominican preacher, Father Lacordaire, who entered the National Assembly in 1848 as a deputy wearing his monk's robe, and cried out, when angry voices were raised: "Cette robe est une liberté."—Others were the famous Bishop of Orleans, Monseigneur Dupanloup, who was as pious as he was intellectually distinguished; the philosopher, Père Gratry, and, among the laymen, Count Falloux, Augustin Cochin, and others. No judgment was ever pronounced in Rome concerning this conflict, but it was known that the tendency then prevailing there inclined to favour Montalembert's opponents. What the latter wanted was simply for the Church to take her place in the unceasing movement of our times towards freedom, and in this atmosphere of liberty to build rather on her own moral power than on the protection of earthly authorities, for which she had always paid dearly. From the practical point of view, moreover, this was the only possible thing to do. Montalembert preferred the Church to strike out boldly on these lines rather than waste time in fruitless lamentations. As I have said, this controversy is now completely settled, and a balance has been struck between

47

the immutability of Christian teaching and the necessary adjustment to changing external circumstances. I am happy to put it on record that my Church stands to-day at the head of social progress, instead of appearing to seek salvation in a past which can never return, and whose conditions can hardly be described as ideal. At Montalembert's house I met Père Gratry and Monsieur Augustin Cochin, whom I have already mentioned. The latter had presented himself as a candidate for one of the Paris constituencies, and was only narrowly beaten. I was present at some of his election meetings, and was always glad to take part in gatherings of this kind. On the *impériales* of the omnibuses, which were in those days the favourite means of transport in Paris—and admirable they were in their way—I used to start political discussions with working men. This was to some extent unwise, because it was easy to be taken for a police spy and to be treated accordingly. Fortunately, nothing of the kind happened to me, and I left Paris with every kind of instructive impression. I took with me also an ardent admiration for the great, sick man who had opened the way for me to so much, and with whom I, though an immature boy, was yet to exchange a few letters.

The winter of the following year brought with it one of the most interesting spiritual experiences of my youth. I stayed in Rome for several weeks at a time when the Vatican Council was sitting. There was great excitement

48

about the expected declaration of the infallibility of the Pope. Opinion was divided even in strict Catholic circles and among the most prominent ecclesiastics, not so much concerning the problem itself as to whether it was advisable to place it on the agenda. People whom the controversy did not concern also insisted on taking part in it. Among these I count all those who stood outside the Catholic faith, as, considered dispassionately, it must have been a matter of complete indifference to them whether the gift of infallibility on questions of faith belonged only to the Pope and his Council in common, or also to the Pope alone. From a common-sense point of view, the infallibility of an assembly is as absurd as that of a single man. To the one, as to the other, infallibility can only be granted through an act of divine grace which is assured to the Church according to our faith. In the spirit of this faith, it is just as reasonable that the gift should be granted to one man as to an assembly, for in both cases it comes only from divine assistance, and not from the greater or lesser abilities of men. The eager participation of the non-Catholic world in this controversy, and the attitude which it took up against papal infallibility, had therefore no logical foundation, and only betrayed a desire to harm the authority of the Church.

All the activities of diplomats swarming around the Council, by which certain governments even hoped to

influence its decision, seemed to me then—as it does now—
equally unjustified. Worldly powers, in particular the
Holy Roman Emperors, had, in fact, interfered in the
affairs of earlier Councils—to mention only the Council
of Constance. This had even then led to bad results,
though it can be explained to a certain extent by the close
relationship which formerly bound Church and State
together. In our time, when this relationship no longer
holds, interference is completely unjustifiable. In this
instance, the Church strictly forbade the intrusion of the
temporal power, but it is most regrettable that a small
group in the Church party, which opposed the suggested
dogmatic declaration, was not equally decisive in its
resistance. Opposition as such, and the defence of a conviction, whether dogmatic or opportunist, about a problem
not yet officially regulated by the Church, was the right,
and indeed the duty, of the Fathers in Council; they had
been summoned to deliver judgment to the best of their
ability. There was therefore no cause to look askance at,
and to criticise, the Bishops who were against the declaration of infallibility, as did certain over-zealous individuals.
Men like Dupanloup and Ketteler, with the majority of
German, Austrian and Hungarian Bishops, belonged to
the party that withstood the new dogma. This fact, and
also my relations with Montalembert's circle, caused me
to come in frequent contact with these Bishops, who
entered into confidential discussions with me. One day,

a prominent Catholic layman, who was a keen supporter of the infallibility doctrine, gave me a fatherly warning, and spoke to me in the tone which an older man adopts towards a younger who has got into bad company. I could not help regarding this fatherly admonition as one of those comic episodes which so often accompany serious events. My personal point of view was that which I still hold to be right, and the only fitting one for a layman— namely, to await the decision of the Church with patience, and then to accept it with faith. I thought it inappropriate to take sides beforehand, nor did I feel the slightest right to do so.

Such great prelates as I was able to approach, I met without considering their attitude in the infallibility question. I had many serious conversations with Monseigneur Dupanloup about the general position of the Catholic Church. During these talks he listened with great patience to my precocious opinions, and corrected them from the rich store of his experience. He was equally gifted as a pedagogue, a Church historian, and an astute politician, and he exercised a considerable influence over his generation. As a contrast, I should like to mention one of the heads of the infallibility party, Dr. Henry Manning, afterwards Cardinal Archbishop of Westminster. He and Cardinal Newman were the chief surviving members of a Catholic group in the Anglican Church which started the Oxford Movement in the forties of last century. Both men entered the Catholic Church after a severe spiritual struggle, though they were destined to achieve great eminence. Newman I only know from his writings; his was a personality quite different from Manning's, being more akin to the French "Liberal Catholics." Manning, on the other hand, was a powerful, harmonious character, an enemy to all compromise, and one who always put principle above opportunist considerations. And yet his efforts to establish the position of the Catholic Church in England were rewarded by great practical success. The integrity of his character, which compelled admiration, was chiefly to thank for this, though it was assisted by an intimate friendship that had existed between him and Gladstone since their Oxford days. This friendship was not injured when they chose to follow separate paths in religious matters. Manning honoured me several times by an exchange of views, although he knew to which party I was inclined, for he was far above allowing this to affect the kindness which he always showed me. He fully approved of my view that it was best to await the decision of the Church with patience. His reputation in the Church was so great that he was often spoken of as the future Pope, and I could only have welcomed it as a piece of good fortune if a non-Italian had once more occupied the throne.

The great Bishop of Mainz, Freiherr von Ketteler, attracted me most of all. He also showed me such kindness that I discussed with him everything which seemed to me difficult, or caused me anxiety. He gave me many valuable lessons in matters that were of interest to my newly acquainted public conscience, for the social reform movement in the Catholic Church originated with him. He sought out any source of information from which he might learn something, and everyone knows of his friendship with Lassalle. My conversations with this enlightened prince of the Church strengthened me in the conviction, which I had already reached, that we need never be in doubt as to the truth even if its representatives occasionally pay their tribute to human weakness. Indeed, the period of great moral corruption in the highest Church circles offers one of the strongest arguments, not against, but for the supernatural character of her authority, for she never erred in dogmatic decisions even when her human agents were at their worst.

The summit of the building—if I may call the spiritual results of my stay in Rome a building—was my audience with Pope Pius IX. He received me with all the paternal kindness and charm radiating from his personality, which silenced any inclination to criticism. This was so at least in the case of a believing Catholic, such as I was and still remain. For a faithful Catholic it is always impossible to approach the supreme head of his Church without being deeply moved, even when he has so small a share of humility as I had when young. The school of ecclesiastical policy to which I was attracted was not that which enjoyed the favour of Pius IX. It is well known what experiences had served to make him mistrust all modern intellectual tendencies and political movements. When he ascended the papal throne in 1847, he was, politically speaking—if I may use this expression for the sake of brevity—the most advanced Liberal who had ever occupied that high position. He wanted to leave the government of the Papal State entirely to lay hands, and to introduce constitutional rule. The experiment was an absolute failure, no doubt because it took place in the *Sturm und Drang* period of Italian national awakening, and because it coincided with the revolutionary wave then sweeping across Europe. This disappointment caused the young Pope completely to change his ideas. His Pontificate became one of the most conservative, and he not only allied himself with the world reaction which everywhere followed the movements of 1848, but was regarded as one of its main supporters. Much, therefore, separated my mentality from his own, but, over and above this, was the consciousness of his great spiritual distinction and of the venerable, kindly figure in which this was embodied. I left the Holy Father with a serene feeling of child-like reverence, and the impression gained at this audience was strengthened a few days later on Easter Sunday at the religious celebrations in St. Peter's. The Holy Father himself officiated at High Mass, surrounded by the Bishops of the entire world, in that colossal house of God whose vastness is a symbol of the universal Church. Pius IX was essentially what one would call a "decorative" high priest. Tall and upright, with a handsome, expressive face, and a fine, musical voice which carried without effort across any room, he offered the Holy Sacrament in a manner that must have moved everyone. In the midst of the service, the deathly stillness of the overcrowded Cathedral was broken by a subdued music of trumpets in the dome. One had an almost unearthly impression, which was deepened by the consciousness of its essential dignity and of absolute surrender to the mystery of the sacrifice.

I was still in Rome when the Council made its declaration of Papal infallibility. Two votes were cast against it, and a number of Bishops refrained from voting, but when the decision was announced, they all declared they would accept it. Only a group of scientists stood aloof, among whom there were incontestably some brilliant men—I need only mention Dr. Döllinger, Provost of the Collegiate Church at Munich. To my mind, their action was inconsistent, for they had always recognised the infallibility of the Pope in associations with the Council, yet they were now opposing just such a decision. But this is a matter which they must settle with their own consciences. It is enough for me to note the utter failure of that "Old Catholic" movement, which was launched with such pomp, and for a while aroused great expectations even in Bismarck. It was obvious that this movement would fail, because our age is consistent in that it offers a fruitful soil for unbelief, but not for heresy. A man either believes in the divine assistance enjoyed by dignitaries of the Church, in which case it is logically impossible to reject any of their decisions, or he does not believe it, and therefore they are all meaningless to him—but in this case he has no claim to be a Catholic. The total effect of diverse, and sometimes disturbing impressions which I had received during my stay in Rome was a harmonious one. In all its grandeur, the imposing and indestructible unity of my Church rose up before me.

Every trace has vanished of the dissensions and clashes within the Catholic Church which have been the subject of this present chapter. This fact is the most interesting of all. Such controversies are still worthy of mention to-day, because they form the background of a great historical phenomenon; at no time since the foundation of the Catholic Church has its unity been so complete as in our day. The faithful see in this fact the mastery of God's Providence, which makes unity more secure when it is most needed. From a human standpoint two factors have chiefly contributed to this achievement—the personality of the Popes who have held office during the last half-century, each of whom has been distinguished in his own way, and the intellectual tendency of our time, which either completely accepts or flatly denies the authority of the Church. Another point is that Church unity has received considerable help from the technical achievements of modern science. The Church has every reason to welcome these, and to encourage their advance. The help she receives from them was symbolically expressed when Pope Pius XI spoke to the whole world, and Marconi, standing beside the Holy Father, received his blessing. How much more difficult it was in days gone by for a universal Church to carry out the duties of teacher, and to maintain discipline, when it took many weeks, or even months, for the news of a hostile intellectual movement to reach Rome, and as many weeks or months for corrective measures to be put into force! Nowadays, what happens in Helsingfors in the morning is known in Rome by the evening. The next day, all necessary instructions are received in Helsingfors, while the further progress of the matter can be influenced from hour to hour. In this way, no interval is allowed for the unchecked growth of the mischief, which can be detected at once, and remedied in so far as it is capable of cure.

If I compare the present position of the Papacy—its authority within the Church, its external influence and the power it wields—with that obtaining in my youth, I observe an enormous increase, about which one may hold various opinions, but which an impartial investigation cannot deny. And this has come to pass in the twentieth century of its existence, after it has surmounted terrific attacks from without and trials from within! A fact, this, which must set everybody thinking. So long as one is free from anti-clerical passions and prejudices, one need not even be a Catholic to see in this strengthening of the moral power represented by the Papacy a factor in the play of historical forces which is important to all mankind. As against this, we are threatened with the spectre of Bolshevism, an avowed and systematic revolt, carried through with vigour, skill, and fanaticism, against the divine ordering of the world. Whoever does not wish to join this revolt, and to see the victory of this enemy of mankind, must welcome the strengthening of that moral force which is best organised to withstand the foe.

The journeys of which I have spoken, and to which I must add a third, to Egypt in the autumn of 1869, were mere episodes in the steady, methodical, intellectual work of those years. The greater part of my time was taken up with studies at Eberhard, and these were chiefly concerned with economics and sociology. My library bears the stamp of that period, for never since have I had leisure to read so much, or to buy so many books. But now, when I look through my bookcases, I have a sensation such as one experiences on examining the books of a past century in some old castle, when one tries with their help to revive the mental atmosphere of a generation that is no more. Most of the books which were regarded as classics in the sixties and early seventies of the last century, and which served as a basis for my studies, are almost as out of date now as those of still earlier generations. My generation belongs to the past, and while I cannot help having been a member of it, I must endeavour not to appear too unlike the present one. I cannot claim that this is very difficult for me. The transition is symbolised by my having Wilhelm Roscher and Werner Sombart next to each other in my library. Already at the time when Roscher was my oracle, I had a presentiment of certain ideas towards which I was unconsciously working, and whose most complete expression is to be found in Werner Sombart's monumental work on capitalism. I was enthralled by the grandeur of the system which Roscher's thought and massive logic had built up. This system rested upon the idea of the free interplay of all economic forces producing a natural balance, and upon that of the harmony of interests. Even in the first phase of my studies, I suspected that all was not well with this theory, that the production of commodities was regarded too much as an end in itself, and that men were hardly taken into account. The greater part of mankind was looked upon exclusively, or at least chiefly, as something to be reckoned among the costs of production, like the price of coal or the interest paid on invested capital. Such a conception of the place of Labour in the economic system aroused my immediate opposition, for it was entirely separated from the moral value inherent in every human being, and from the claims arising therefrom being put on a level with any material commodity. I could not silence my doubts, nor did Marx, on the other hand, offer me any satisfying solution. Responsible capitalist enterprise seemed indispensable to me then, as it does to-day, not only for the security and efficient supervision of work, but for the necessary differentiation according to ability, and therefore for progress in general. I was mentally prepared for the social reform theories which soon made themselves felt in science. In this, Bishop Ketteler strengthened and encouraged me. I found these movements reconcilable with my religious faith, and my thought developed further on such lines. The whole of my political activity in after-years is a witness to this, though my attention was distracted by other problems just at the critical moment. It is strange how single sentences in the works which I read at this stage of my sociological and economic study, suddenly illuminated important truth, and provoked changes in my thought. When I took up for the first time Schäffle's book on economics, then considered a very advanced work, the reading of his table of contents affected me in this way. The book was divided into two parts, with the sub-titles "The system of private enterprise" and "The system of communal enterprise in human economy." It flashed into my mind that the selfish motive of private enterprise was not the only one in economic life, and, for its better understanding, motives of collective enterprise must also be reckoned with. Later my Free Trade convictions received a sudden shock from which they never recovered when I read this sentence in Friedrich List:—"Free Trade is the system of exchange value; Protection that of active producing forces."—I am only speaking of single moments, but these were the starting points for important tendencies in the development of my thought.

When I sat for the examination in political science in the autumn of 1870, I thought myself so conversant with the subject of the examination that I had the effrontery to start a scientific argument with the economic examiner, Gyula Kauz, a very capable professor, and afterwards my respected colleague in Parliament. He asked me a question about which I had already made up my mind in a different sense from that expounded in the Professor's textbook. I answered the question according to his book, but remarked that I did not agree with the opinion there maintained. The Professor asked me why I stressed this, so, for better or worse, I was obliged to acknowledge my convictions, and, at his request, I gave him my views. Professor Kauz—to his honour—took this unusual behaviour in a very friendly spirit, only saying that he would not then argue about the different conceptions, as he was satisfied that I had made a thorough study of the problem. Moreover, he gave me a special distinction.

I came of age in 1870. There was no longer anything to hinder me from entering public life and taking up the career in Parliament which I was planning, except my own conviction that I was not yet ripe for it. I wanted to see more of the world, especially of England, which I had never visited, but which, as a budding Parliamentarian with ambitions, I considered the paragon that should be studied before all others. I regret that I had no chance to do so. My whole acquaintance with the constitutional tradition of England, and with those of her heroes whom I admired, had to be gathered from books. In 1872, equipped thus slenderly, as it seemed to me, I entered Parliament, of which I have been a member, with one short interval, ever since.

CHAPTER III

LISZT AND WAGNER

Music, the art of pure emotion, has played a quite unique role in my life. I am neither a creative musician, nor a performer, nor even versed in musical theory, but merely susceptible to its gifts. This is the case to such an extent that music forms an intrinsic part of my life, and has influenced my whole personality. That applies also to my political activity. Of course, I have never tried to find the solution to a tariff problem, or difficult point of constitutional or international law in Sebastian Bach or in Mozart, in Beethoven or in Richard Wagner. But I have felt quite clearly that the influence of the greatest—but only of the greatest—music has increased my perceptive powers, and also my facility for surveying and grasping some question, even of politics, in its entirety.

This profound attachment to the art of music originated during my years in Kalksburg. In early childhood, I enjoyed ordinary piano lessons, the only purely mechanical part of my upbringing—if I can use the word enjoyment in such a connection. These lessons bored me to death, especially the insipid drawing-room pieces which I had to

63

learn, like other children in the same plight, for birthdays and feast-days. When I went to Kalksburg, the piano was among the minor subjects taught. I looked forward with resignation to that half-hour three times a week. As it turned out, a teacher took me in hand whose conception and method wrought a complete change. He was an unassuming Bohemian musician, named Franz Frey, no great virtuoso, but a man well grounded in the theory of music, and filled with a glowing enthusiasm for the art into which he had to initiate a lot of ungrateful boys. In me he found an appreciative pupil, and I mention his name because this modest, and in no way prominent, but nevertheless efficient and conscientious man was a determining influence in my education. I remember, as if it had been yesterday, how in the first lesson I had with him he was trying to gauge the extent of my knowledge. I had played over to him one or other of the drawing-room pieces in my repertory, when he thought for a moment, and then said:—"Look here, we aren't going to waste our time with that sort of stuff. I'm going to introduce you to classical music."—With these words, he laid the Adagio from Beethoven's Pathetic Sonata on the piano, played it to me and bade me try my own hand at it, a task in which I proved fairly competent. But that is not the principal thing. The impression it made on me was one of utter bewilderment in face of a new world that opened before me. Further and ever further I advanced, for each hour at the piano was also an hour of musical discussion, an introduction of the fourteen-year-old boy into the heart of great musical creations. Frey was enthusiastic about Richard Wagner, which was nothing remarkable in those days; but I am speaking now of the early sixties, when Hanslick was still supreme in Viennese musical criticism, and "Wagnerite" was equivalent with crank. I remember a piano lesson which my teacher gave me after he had been in Vienna and had heard *Lohengrin*. That day there was no real lesson, but only torrential outbursts of enthusiasm about the master's greatest work, and of faith in his epoch-making mission.

In this way I gathered what I might call intellectual impressions of music, since I had as yet had no opportunity of hearing any major works. My head was full of these impressions when I entered upon the first two years of my University life in Vienna. There I could satisfy the craving for musical knowledge to my heart's content. As a matter of fact, I spent three years—1863 to 1866—studying in Vienna, for, as I have already explained in another connection, I devoted a year exclusively to philosophical studies after matriculating. During these years, almost the only pleasures that I allowed myself in the intervals of my studies were musical. Listening and reflecting, I took in all that opera, philharmonic and society concerts, chamber music and the performances of great virtuosos had to give me. Strangely enough, I never became personally acquainted with any of the great artists whose performances I enjoyed. Those were the days when Hellmesberger, of whom I was an enthusiastic admirer, and Laub, were rivals in Viennese chamber music, when the pianists Clara Schumann, Karl Tausig and so modern a player as Rubinstein were most admired; Herbeck was head of the "Friends of Music" Society, and, at the Opera House, the great tenor Ander was still enjoying the twilight of his fame. It was always said that he had no voice left, but his perfect singing of *Lohengrin* I will never forget. I was a stranger to all these stars in the musical heaven, a fact which may perhaps have favoured the independent growth of my musical appreciation.

And now I pass on with one bound to the time when, already intellectually mature, I was able to meet in person the greatest living geniuses of music, and when, thanks to them, my appreciation could fully develop. These years coincide with my entry into public life and—what is more important—with the great Hungarian renaissance that set in after the *Ausgleich* of 1867.

At the end of the sixties and the beginning of the seventies, Ferencz Liszt began to spend a part of each year in Budapest. He was free from all engagements, and seemed anxious to devote most of his energy to the fostering of music in his own land, for his heart had always remained true to Hungary. There was talk of founding an Academy of Music in Budapest, and of placing Ferencz

Liszt at its head. The world-famous political philosopher, Baron József Eötvös, then Minister of Education, took up the idea, and it was seriously discussed with Ferencz Liszt. I was, of course, enthusiastic about the plan from the beginning, and sought an opportunity to meet Liszt. How this came to pass I no longer remember. Our relations at first were of a commonplace, social kind. He could have no insight into my mind, and could not detect all the enthusiasm for music which was stirring in me, and especially for the type of music whose chief representative, after Wagner, was himself. Nor do I recall how and when the ice was broken between us. I know only that the friendship which was developing at that time between Ödön Mihálovich and myself certainly helped to bring us nearer together. Mihálovich, that very gifted young musician, afterwards played a great part in the musical development of Hungary, and was already a keen admirer of Wagner and Liszt. He stood to both of them in that personal relationship of pupil to master which is so difficult to define.

Through Mihálovich I saw more of Ferencz Liszt, and from time to time I was invited to join his own circle. We became friends as a result of my efforts, first in the newspapers, and then as a young member of Parliament, in favour of establishing the Academy of Music.

When I entered Parliament in 1872, I found this affair in a very bad way. During budgetary discussions, the previous Parliament, for reasons of economy, had cancelled the sum put aside by the Minister of Education to establish an Academy. The same fate threatened this item when the Ministry of Education placed it in the budget of 1873. I made up my mind to speak publicly in its favour. It was my maiden speech in the Hungarian Parliament, and I should like to think it characteristic, or shall we say symbolical, that it was made in the cause of music. This is not the place to describe what a maiden speech means to an ambitious young member, nor the political complications which made it still more important for me. It is enough to say that my position in the House was far from being secure, depending as it did on the good-will shown to me by Ferencz Deák, the leader of Parliament, and of the Hungarian nation. He took an obvious interest in my first speech, and this must be why it resulted in a complete success, not only for me personally but for the cause which I was defending. The sum was voted by an overwhelming majority, and I may add that my position in Parliament was secured.

Nevertheless, there were still some set-backs in this affair. On December 4, 1874, Liszt wrote to me concerning the Academy of Music: "The Government has taken up this matter in earnest. A decision was even obtained from the King, but I do not know what official announcement followed. You yourself, my dear Count, brilliantly persuaded Parliament that the Academy was necessary for the development of the art in Hungary. My humble but necessary observations have been universally taken as a sign of assent. Should we be right to ignore all these occurrences and simply give way, when we ought to be pressing forward? I think not, and am of your opinion, which seems to me as wise as it is timely. Despite the obstacles thrown in our way by various reverses, and despite slender financial backing, we must abide by our affirmative point of view, and not yield. As regards my personal wishes, in which you take a friendly interest, allow me to assure you once more that I am striving towards a single goal: peace to work in my own room. *Orare et laborare!* It is a point of honour which draws me to Hungary, our Fatherland, and no one understands this better than you. Once there, I could really discharge all my debts of gratitude."

This first episode in my Parliamentary career drew my personal relations with Ferencz Liszt closer day by day. Liszt then had a modest flat on the Fischplatz, which has completely disappeared in the course of town-planning. In the evening, I would often meet a little group of friends there from the Budapest world of music. Sometimes they had come to supper, which at Liszt's always consisted of cold dishes, and which he called "cold treatment." There were always stimulating and instructive conversations. In the course of them, Liszt would often take his seat at the piano, perhaps to illustrate his words, and the enviable

69

members of that circle would hear fragments of Beethoven or Mozart sonatas played in the most spontaneous manner, untrammelled by any thought of a public. Those were real courses in musical history. It was understood that we should not ask Liszt to play. Whoever did so, fell from grace and spoilt the atmosphere of the whole evening: it had to be done at his own suggestion. I was a constant guest at these evening gatherings, where I felt, to a certain extent, like Saul among the prophets. Other famous artists used also to come there, musicians who had visited Budapest to pay their respects to Liszt, even if they were not giving a concert. These naturally took an active part in the musical performances, but they all sat as pupils at Liszt's feet, and listened to his every word as if it were the saying of an oracle. Among them were some of the greatest—Rubinstein, Paderewski, and among famous violinists, Wieniawski and others. Of course, the real pupils, and the young pianists and violinists, were at these gatherings, too. Liszt was plagued by talented and un-talented musicians who sought his advice and help, for the gift of ridding himself of the failures was never his.

Now that I was able to observe Liszt almost daily in his own circle, there grew up, beside the admiration which I felt for the artist, genuine esteem and affection for the man. He was not without his faults. The seed of vanity which sprouts in every man could not be lacking in him, after an unparalleled career as a virtuoso such as he had enjoyed.

This asserted itself sometimes in a way that detracted from his dignity. But he was a noble and good man, one of the best I have ever known. Jealousy and ill-will were unknown to him. How many musicians became known through Liszt, and owe any recognition they met with to the publicity he gave them! It was an immense satisfaction to him to discover talent, and anyone who wished to make serious progress in music always found him actively encouraging. I would stress this absence of jealousy in his character, because I have never met with it to such a degree in any man of importance having rivals in his own field. The close friendship which had united him in earlier years with Chopin is a proof of this. It did not exclude an occasional shaft of malice about his equals—but only about them. The following little story illustrates this. He told it me himself, perhaps thirty years after it had happened, with an obvious pleasure at the success of his joke. When his fame as a virtuoso was at its height, in the forties of last century, Liszt was staying for a while in Paris at the same time as Chopin. One evening they both took part in a musical soirée, at the house of some great lady. On that occasion, Liszt had the feeling that Chopin had put him in the shade, and in spite of their friendship, this irritated him. Then he had a brilliant idea. While Chopin was sitting at the piano and playing magnificently, Ferencz Liszt crept up to the hostess and whispered to her that it would be interesting to hear Chopin in the dark.

Would she not have the lights put out? As soon as this had been done, Liszt slipped into the chair next to Chopin, and whispered that he should let him go on playing. Chopin entered into the joke, and, without anyone noticing, Liszt took over from him the musical phrases which had already begun, and played his piece through to the end. Nobody suspected what had happened, and there was boundless amazement among the people when the lights were lit again, and they saw Liszt sitting at the piano. Standing up, the latter said to Chopin:—"My dear Frederick, just do me a favour by sitting down at the piano, and playing so as to make the people think that it's Liszt!"—This harmless joke, with which Liszt had procured a satisfaction from his friend and rival that would otherwise have been denied him, did not in the least disturb their friendly relations. Liszt took pleasure in this anecdote all his life, just as anyone of us might enjoy recalling some harmless but successful prank of youth.

His fame was already secure in most parts of Europe. King William III of Holland was in the habit of inviting the greatest artists of the time to his Court, so as to give representatives of the most diverse arts a chance to meet while enjoying Royal hospitality. Liszt was often invited to these interesting gatherings. On several occasions, he wrote me an account of them, and mentioned by name the painters who had been invited, such as Potaels, Hamman, Ten Kate, Rochussen, Heemskerk, and such musicians as

Ambroise Thomas, composer of *Hamlet* and *Mignon* and director of the Paris Conservatoire, the famous violinist Wieniawski, and others. In the evening, there were always lectures at the Dutch Court on the history of art, music, and so forth. Liszt wrote to me about one of these visits on May 8, 1875:—"There is no one present beyond the guests personally admitted by His Majesty, hardly more than twenty in all. Even at meals, no woman is present, nor even a maid. The fair sex shines by its absence, and this sometimes benefits the ugly sex without injuring the ladies."

It was a fashion then, and long afterwards, to admire in Ferencz Liszt only the pianist, and to disparage the composer. It is quite otherwise now, and, from the very first, the great impression which many of Liszt's works produced on me, convinced me that this verdict was unjust. It must be admitted that in the mass of his output there is some indifferent work of an ephemeral kind; but is not this the case with every creative artist who fills many volumes, either of poetry or of music? Is everything supremely great in the thirty-odd volumes of Goethe's works? Have we not mediocre products even of Beethoven's muse? The capacity of a creative mind is to be reckoned from its greatest achievement. And what treasures we find amongst the music which Ferencz Liszt has bequeathed to us! I will only mention the Dante and Faust symphonies, the piano concertos and sonatas, a few of the songs, the Esztergom and coronation masses, and the oratorios *Elizabeth* and *Christus*. The last especially contains ideas as profound as the finest religious music ever written. I would remind those who know this rarely played work of the section which introduces the eight Beatitudes from the Sermon on the Mount as they are recorded in St. Matthew's gospel. The writing of a musical commentary to this text, unique in the literature of the world, was the greatest task which a deep-thinking, cultured, religious musician, who was at the same time a genius, could set himself. And how superbly Liszt has achieved it! He uses the simplest possible means to attain his end—a baritone solo, a mixed chorus, and organ or harmonium accompaniment. With these he builds up a psychological unity, and brings home to us the baffling effect of the new doctrine on the masses. These Beatitudes seemed a complete paradox according to current ideas: the poor in spirit, the meek, the humble, the merciful, those that are pure in heart. What a violent contrast to a world founded on the cult of riches, force, and sensuality, not only in practice, as is widely the case even to-day, but on principle and with conviction! While the baritone solo announces the Beatitudes one after the other, as if they were self-evident truths, using only the simplest modulations; with a similar accompaniment the answer of the chorus rings out after each, and symbolises its effect on the audience. This answer is a repetition of the doctrine to which they have just been listening. It comes at first in slow time, with the rhythm but slightly accentuated, and expresses a struggle going on in their minds about the paradox which they have heard. Passing from Beatitude to Beatitude, the entry of the chorus becomes more definite, more powerful, and more impressive. You feel the spirit unfolding, the heart gathering warmth, knowledge increasing. The greatest of all paradoxes resounds from the mouth of the Saviour: "Blessed are they that have been persecuted for righteousness' sake,"—and these words are expressed in a simple but marvellously effective ascending third; then the echo of the chorus bursts out with joyful certainty. Their spiritual battle is won. The greatest decision which has ever been taken in world history here finds a musical expression of a clarity and power such as only the greatest genius in its finest work can show us.

It is difficult, if not impossible, to describe in words the feelings and impressions which music awakens. If it were otherwise, music would not be what it is. It is the expression of something that passes understanding, that goes deeper than all metaphysics, and that everyone must experience for himself.

Ferencz Liszt grew up at a time when his genius could not be given a worthy musical education in Hungary. There was no Academy of Music where an artist, striving to reach the heights, could obtain the necessary teaching and indispensable guidance. There was no public musically cultured and experienced enough to influence a young artist, or even to guarantee him a livelihood. Vienna, on the other hand, which lay so close to Ferencz Liszt's home in the county of Sopron, was the recognised musical capital of Europe, giving access to the whole musical world of Germany with its educational facilities. It is small wonder that the young Liszt left his native land in order to study, and did not return there to put his art as a virtuoso into practice. Nevertheless, he had absorbed the themes of Hungarian folk music, and was able to make use of them as only one born to understand them could do. We need only compare the manner in which he introduces Hungarian themes into the oratorio *Elizabeth*, without robbing them of their national flavour, and also his Hungarian rhapsodies with the beautiful, but intensely German, Hungarian Dances of Brahms, to realise that Ferencz Liszt's work is a genuine product of the Hungarian spirit, and that it is no pretension, but an undeniable fact, when we claim him as our own. He always wanted to be a Hungarian, and to be known as such. A man does not cease to belong to his native land and to embody its typical qualities because he absorbs the intellectual treasures of an entire world, and wields an influence over all mankind.

It is no far cry from Liszt to Wagner. Through Liszt, I met that great man, and thanks to my friendship with my compatriot, I had the entrée to the Villa Wahnfried, which

was not a common privilege. Certain impressions that
mark the highest point of my musical experience belong
inseparably to my recollection of these two, with whom
there associated in spirit a Titan from the realm of the
dead—namely, Beethoven.

I had formed a theoretical admiration for Wagner through
my music master at Kalksburg before I ever heard a note of
his work. My first opportunity to do this came when I had
left Kalksburg and made Vienna my headquarters for the
next three years. By chance on the very evening when my
parents got into their new home in Vienna during the
winter of 1863–64, *Lohengrin* was being performed in the
Court Opera House, which was still called the Kärtnertor-
theater. Eagerly I hastened to the performance, and
my heart beat violently with anticipation. But a strong
musical impression was all that I carried away during these
years, though I heard *Lohengrin, Tannhäuser* and the
Flying Dutchman fairly often. The importance and real
meaning of Wagner's work, its conscious and unconscious
philosophical content, had not as yet revealed itself to my
mind. This happened for the first time in Bayreuth, and it
took decades for my appreciation to mature and crystal-
lise. Up to *Parsifal*, my understanding was still frag-
mentary. I only appreciated all the nuances of Wagner
thanks to this work, and then only after prolonged study.
During the years in Vienna, I had not advanced beyond a
rather commonplace admiration of those three works

which were known to me. *Tristan* had so far never been performed outside Munich, and even Wagner admirers on my rudimentary level of understanding accepted the almost universal dictum of the critics, that this work was "unproducible" and "tedious." The present generation can hardly realise that for years this opinion prevailed.

I learnt a little more from Ferencz Liszt, groping my way slowly at first, for I did not feel the need to discuss Richard Wagner theoretically with him. I knew, indeed, the two wonderful essays on *Lohengrin* and *Tannhäuser* with which Liszt had prepared the way of the first performance of those works, conducted by himself at the Weimar Hoftheater in the fifties. Liszt would often talk about the difficulties of that performance, and used to enjoy telling us how he felt when he first read through the text. He found himself face to face with an utterly new phenomenon in the world of opera. Admiringly, he would speak of Wagner's dramatisation, and his musical portrayal of great problems of ethics and psychology. He told how it had delighted and thrilled him to study the scores which so great a genius as Richard Wagner had elaborated out of the vast world of his thought. With a touching humility, he bowed before him as being the greater, never questioning Wagner's pre-eminence as a creative artist, but acknowledging it almost ostentatiously, adding at the same time in his humorous way:—"All the same, my fingering on the piano is better." This was not saying much, for Richard Wagner had no claims as a virtuoso. His greatest amusement at the piano was to play, more or less badly, the Strauss waltzes which he loved.

Once, when Richard Wagner came to Budapest, he partook of a quiet luncheon with Ferencz Liszt, Frau Cosima, Mihálovich, my cousin Sándor Apponyi and myself. We had brought my cousin, although he was not such a musical enthusiast as I was; yet he could admire what was great in music, and was so intelligent and widely cultured that he was at home among intellectuals of any kind. His presence was welcomed by Richard Wagner, who enjoyed talking to him. They left the dining-room of the hotel in conversation and went up to Wagner's room together. Sándor Apponyi entered and found there a piano on which stood the open music of Johann Strauss's *Blue Danube*. The conversation must have turned to this, for Wagner sat down at the piano and played a few bars of the immortal *Danube* Waltz, enthusiastically praising its beauty. I envied my cousin this experience: it is not everyone who can hear Richard Wagner playing Strauss. This admiration for Strauss, which I heartily endorsed, is very characteristic of Wagner's attitude to other musicians. As a contrast to Liszt, who was able to appreciate everything, Richard Wagner's own personality always influenced his judgment of other composers. His highest admiration was reserved for those who stood completely outside his own sphere, and whom he could criticise quite objectively. Hence his appreciative words about the old-style Italian operas, and his joy in Johann Strauss. His supreme veneration of Beethoven arose out of the nature of Beethoven's art, which was spiritual and removed from all subjective impulses. I once saw the proud head of Richard Wagner bowed in deep humility before Beethoven, and nothing has moved me more than this homage by genius to the greatness which he felt himself unable to reach. I have also seen flashes of self-criticism on the part of Richard Wagner which belong to the most interesting psychological experiences in my recollection. My mental picture of this man is very different from that usually drawn.

I first met Richard Wagner in Weimar at Ferencz Liszt's house. It must have been in the first half of the seventies. The occasion was a first performance of the oratorio *Christus*, which took place in the Protestant church under the direction of the Grand Duke's conductor, Eduard Lassen. Richard Wagner had come to this performance, and we three from Budapest, Mihálovich, János Végh and I, were among the immense crowd of spectators. Végh was an intimate friend of us both. An excellent connoisseur of music, he was a judge by profession, and a sensitive, kindly man. We made a travelling trio, and constantly visited towns where unusual musical performances were to be heard.

I have already given my views on the oratorio. The

distinguished audience was deeply impressed by it. After the first performance, the next day perhaps, Ferencz Liszt invited those of the visitors whom he knew intimately to a meal, and on this occasion I was introduced to Richard Wagner. With a trembling heart, I advanced to meet the demi-god. As one might have expected, this first encounter was confined to an exchange of banalities, and so things stood for the time being, for Wagner left Weimar at once, while we three remained for some time with Ferencz Liszt, and visited the beauty spots of Thüringen, in particular the Wartburg.

Ferencz Liszt was again in the foreground at my next meeting with Wagner, and, this time, the two great living geniuses were joined by a third, invisible but affecting them by his magic spell—namely, Beethoven. Preparations were going on for the opening of the Bayreuth theatre, but the undertaking laboured under financial difficulties. To overcome these, Wagner decided, much against his will, to conduct concerts in various German towns, and to introduce extracts from his works, which he hated doing. For example, he conducted the well-known arrangement of the Ouverture and the "Liebestod" from *Tristan*, the funeral music after Siegfried's death from the *Ring*, and various other passages. I do not know how it happened, but one day we were amazed to hear that Budapest had been included in the list of cities where these concerts were to take place. This happened a year before the Bayreuth theatre was opened with the first performance of the *Ring*.

As soon as the Wagner concert was announced in Budapest, opposition immediately arose. Voices were raised in the press, claiming that Budapest was not a German city, and that no defence could be put forward for the attempt to spend Hungarian money on the support of a German undertaking. Enthusiasm for Richard Wagner was not so general among the public of Budapest as it afterwards became. The protests caught on, and tickets for the Wagner concert were selling so badly that we began to fear a fiasco, which would have been very unpleasant for the Master, and not exactly to the credit of our capital. Liszt was informed of the state of things, and he at once said:—"I will play Beethoven's Concerto in E Flat major at the same concert."—On that day when this decision of the Master became known, all the tickets for the concert were sold out; a material and artistic success which no other town could rival was assured. Wagner was deeply touched by this action on the part of his faithful friend, to whom, as I know from experience, he was warmly attached. He never heard about the unpleasant events which led up to it.

[Here it may be of interest to insert a letter written by Richard Wagner to Liszt, who sent a copy of it to the author. Out of modesty Count Apponyi did not include it in this book.—*Publisher's note*.]

"DEAR FRIEND,

"It seems to me that I owe you a complete and formal letter of thanks. I have an idea that the attitude of deep, friendly understanding which takes it as a mere matter of course is not in itself sufficient. In certain circumstances, one might assume that if we two undertook something together, neither of us would have done any unusual service to the other. As regards our concert in Pest, these circumstances must not be thought to exist, for on that occasion I showed up of necessity as a mere duffer, while you could not do otherwise than appear once more in all your fascinating mastery. I declare that concert in Pest to have been a gift that you made me, and I thank you most heartily for it.

"I also thank your kind friend Count Apponyi, whom I now know and appreciate, as well as the charming Mihálo-vich. They are the only real gains which have come to me through casting my net in Hungary. Give them my heartiest and most respectful greetings.

"I thank you sincerely for your kind forbearance when you released me from the banquet, and graciously said nothing. I am still reproaching myself for not having at once bowed to your wish. The unfriendly resolve to resist was prompted by my obstinate belief that your intercession on behalf of that banquet did not come from your heart. I thought it was rather a concession to circumstances which you have made it a rule of life, but only against your will, to accept, as the most comfortable means of compromising with a world to which both of us must always be strangers. I recognise that I was wrong in not following you with more understanding on this point. Forgive me out of your kindness by remembering the shortcomings and defects of my nature, which you have so often excused in the past.

"In return for that I shall ever bear you more love than you can bear me. If you are always to be kinder-hearted than I must often appear, I shall always surpass you in affection, for this is the share which has fallen to me so that a balance between us may be maintained.

"With all my heart, my noble Franz, I wish you well.

"Yours,

"RICHARD W.

"Bayreuth, March 24, 1875."

Since we are now on the subject of Ferencz Liszt as a virtuoso, another characteristic episode may be mentioned which I did not witness myself, but have from a reliable source. It expresses better than any other the almost incredible musical faculty which Ferencz Liszt possessed. Wagner was once showing him the first sketch of one of his works—I think it was the *Rheingold*. The whole score with complete orchestration had been jotted down. Liszt went straight to a piano, and played the whole work perfectly, without hesitating, as if he had had a piano-setting before him. His glance showed him infallibly, from among the mass of lines and notes, what was essential, picking out at once all that a piano-setting could express. He improvised the piano version, a task which under normal conditions is extremely difficult, as everyone knows who has ever tried. And now back to Budapest.

The concert held there consisted of two parts. In the first, came the Wagner extracts, conducted by the Master himself; in the second, the Beethoven piano concerto, played by Ferencz Liszt and conducted by Hans Richter. We looked forward excitedly to this event, and I must say that Liszt's performance aroused the greatest enthusiasm. His career as a pianist had long since come to an end, and for many years he had refused to appear in public. It was a unique experience to hear him once more playing to crowds of people, now, in his maturity, long since freed from all the dross of virtuosity, the creator of magnificent religious music. For this wonderful experience we had to thank his devoted friendship for Richard Wagner. From the musical point of view, we looked forward to the result with confidence. Our orchestra was even then so highly trained that, suitably conducted, it would prove equal to anything. It was led by Hans Richter, whom Wagner called his "partner," and to whom he had entrusted the first performance of the *Nibelungen*. Richter understood the Budapest orchestra to perfection, and had helped considerably in its development. It was the Master's wish that no one not taking part should be present at the rehearsal which was held on the morning before the performance. Liszt had an exception made to this first rule for my friend Mihálovich and myself, while naturally Frau Cosima was there, and a Herr Jakob Dunkel, who was head of the firm Rózsavölgyi, which arranged the concert, and who was at the same time a sensitive musician. I stress this point because it follows that the atmosphere of the hall was free from any possible disturbance due to some preconceived antagonism, and therefore perfectly adapted for appreciation. I hold this to be a very important point. In my own case, it always upsets me if I feel the presence of someone whom I know to be quite indifferent to what is being played. Nothing of this kind spoilt the atmosphere of the hall in which the rehearsal took place, and I regard that rehearsal as perhaps my greatest musical experience.

I think I am safe in asserting that Ferencz Liszt's playing of the E Flat major Concerto at this rehearsal marked his highest achievement as a pianist, perhaps the highest achievement of which artistic interpretation is capable. As if bewitched, Hans Richter and the orchestra followed the indications of the great Master whom they were privileged to accompany, and in no way did their playing disturb the perfection of the impression, or rather the impression of perfection, which one received from Liszt.

It is now fifty-seven years since I had the experience of hearing Beethoven interpreted by Liszt for Wagner, yet it rings as freshly in my ears and in my mind as though it had been yesterday. One could feel how, at every important turn in that marvellous work, the two living masters, pianist and listener, were in spiritual communion with each other, happy in their common understanding of the dead genius. Invisible threads of suggestion passed from that source of profoundest feeling to us ordinary listeners, and found their way into our grateful and receptive souls. Words fail to describe what we experienced that day. It was simply music, an emotion evoked by sound more glorious than any expressible by thought or speech.

When the rehearsal was over, the few people who had been present went to luncheon together. Not a word was spoken, not a murmur of applause. Everyone felt instinctively that silence alone was befitting the mood in which we were. Richard Wagner had sought out Liszt, and they, too, were silent as they walked from the room. It was only when we were sitting at table that the spell was broken, and Wagner turned excitedly to Liszt with the words:—"My dear Franz, you have beaten me well and truly to-day! What can I do to compare with the playing we have just heard?"—And so the talk went on, with exclamations of humble admiration for Beethoven's genius and of gratitude to Liszt, who could bring it so magically to life. We others had not the courage to intrude upon the conversation. What would have been the good of saying to Liszt:—"Master, you played beautifully to-day"?—All commonplace praise would have been only a profanation of the heights to which we had climbed.

Let us return to earth. The concert took place on the next evening, and in the morning Mihálovich and I went to Liszt's flat to discuss some details with reference to Richard Wagner's stay. To our dismay, we found him with the third finger of his right hand bound up.—"Yes,"—he said smiling,—"as you see, I have cut myself."

We thought there would be no concert now, and asked the Master's opinion.—"Why,"—he answered,—"of course I shall play to-night!"—"And your bad finger?"— "Oh, I shall have to do without it"—was all his reply.

That evening, he actually played the E Flat major Concerto without using the third finger of his right hand, and not a soul detected it! Such was Liszt, the pianist. He played no less wonderfully than on the previous day, but the atmosphere was not so free of hostile influences as it had then been, and I had to wait for an experience which I will describe later before I received another impression comparable to that which the rehearsal had given me.

I cannot say that this visit of Richard Wagner's to Budapest brought me closer to him in a personal sense. He was too busy with the concert, and everything that concerned it, to have time for social activities not directly

connected with his work, even if he had felt drawn to
them. He did speak to me, however, about a much earlier
visit to Budapest, which he had paid at a time when I was
not living there. He recalled an address which had been
delivered on that occasion by my friend Akos Beöthy as
leader of a deputation of young men, and which he
considered one of the most notable demonstrations
ever made on his behalf. Strangely enough, a similar
occurrence was to break the ice between us next year.

As may be supposed, I went to Bayreuth for the three
first cycles of the *Ring der Nibelungen* in the Festival
Theatre. Mihálovich went with me, and we took lodgings
together in a modest house belonging to the town clerk
Nicklas. Conditions of life in Bayreuth were then extra-
ordinarily primitive, and this beautiful Frankish city, seat
of the Margraves of Ansbach and Bayreuth, had difficulty
in rousing itself from the slumber which it had enjoyed for
many decades. All comforts were lacking, the hotels
catered for only the most meagre requirements, and the
means of transport were quite inadequate. This last draw-
back was very unpleasant in bad weather or great heat,
because the Festival Theatre stood some distance from the
centre of the town. There was no drainage, and even years
afterwards, when I was in Bayreuth alone, lodging once
more in a private house, I had always to carry four keys in
my pocket, and fairly large ones at that. The first was the
front-door key, the second the key to my rooms, the third

gave access to the adjoining flat,—it was necessary whenever one wanted to use the fourth. That has all been changed years ago, even before the nineteenth century ended. Drainage has been introduced, while in all private houses where apartments are let you find the most modern sanitation, and at the Festival time there are plenty of taxis, where once only horse carriages were available. The hotels have almost attained the level of those in a big city.

My friend Mihálovich and I were young enough in that first year of the Festival, 1876, to enjoy the comic side of all these provincial shortcomings, which reminded us of the homely comedies of the Kotzebue period. We were amused rather than upset by the inconveniences they entailed. We had been at great pains to equip ourselves with as many changes of linen as we were accustomed to have, and we were amused when the good housewife, who had to look through our laundry, would say, as she took up every article:—"Why, you can still wear that!"—Finally they agreed to accept these eccentricities, and during the three weeks we spent there, the family with whom we lodged took us to their hearts. I was to receive a touching proof of this thirty-five years later. During one of the post-war festivals, an old woman came to see me, bearing a photograph of myself, taken about the time of the first Festival, and assured me she was the daughter of old Nicklas. In the meantime, though she had married, become a mother, a grandmother, and a widow, the memory of those years lived on in her. I confess that I did not remember Fräulein Nicklas, although the family as a whole remained in my memory as a genre-picture of lower middle-class life. With some emotion, I saw that visit resurrected in the person of this old woman.

Above all these little discomforts, rose a sense of the magnificent triumph which Richard Wagner enjoyed at the opening of the Festival Theatre. Though he was still struggling for recognition, and many were the voices raised against him, he had succeeded in building, at a place chosen by himself, a theatre in which he could arrange after his own heart the technical preliminaries for the performances of his masterpiece. He had succeeded also in filling this theatre with a select public, which included the intellectual flower of Germany and distinguished representatives of foreign lands. The campaign was not yet decided, but a major battle had been won. Nearly all the German Princes, with the aged Kaiser Wilhelm at their head, had appeared in acknowledgment of the national character and significance of Wagner's work. He could now proudly survey his achievement, and could labour with renewed creative joy at the completion of his life's work. No one could help observing this. Even his opponents, who had come as professional critics, under the leadership of Hanslick, had to acknowledge the accomplished fact. What must Richard Wagner have felt when the double-basses in the unseen orchestra of the Festival Theatre sounded the first bars of the *Rheingold!*

That I was completely absorbed by the Festival need hardly be said. I was moved and profoundly excited as I took my place at the first performance. The seat beside me was still empty. Imagine my dismay when it was taken by no other than Eduard Hanslick! After what I have said about the influence of counter-suggestions, it will be realised how unpleasantly this meeting affected me. I knew Hanslick slightly, and could not help exchanging a few words with him, though these had nothing to do with Wagner. He knew my opinion, and was tactful not to challenge it. Fortunately, he soon disappeared, I think after the first two performances.

Naturally, faults were to be detected in these renderings, for Wagner had allotted certain roles more with a view to dramatic effect than to quality of singing, and many technical novelties were still untested. Anyone who had come, not with the intention of criticising and acquiring cheap notoriety as a wit, but to enjoy the performance and be uplifted by it, must, however, have gone away richer. The magnificence of Wagner's work impressed itself on you. Its spirit was being given the most perfect expression then possible, thanks to the inspiration of the Master's presence. Nevertheless, if I compare the grasp of his meaning which I then had with the one I believe myself to possess now, I am almost ashamed to look back, so little was I capable of appreciating. However, I took in as much as I could, and that was enough for me.

A remarkable incident came my way in the course of one of the performances. During an interval, my friend Mihálovich wanted to speak to one of the Wagner family, and for this purpose went up into a part of the theatre which was reserved to them. By chance, he entered a room in which he found the Master sitting alone before a writing table and musing. Seeing someone he knew, Wagner rose and said, almost in a tone of discouragement: —"No, that isn't what I imagined. It falls far short of what I intended."—Mihálovich, thinking that the performance was responsible for his dissatisfaction, began to defend it. Wagner answered:—"It's nothing to do with that. I know the people are doing their best; but what I have written is not what lived in my imagination."

This remarkable observation, which throws light on the creative processes of genius, does not in any way lessen the greatness of the creation to which it referred. Genius experiences more than it can reproduce, and inevitably it resents this disproportion between inspiration and the means available for expressing it. Such bitterness would occasionally break out in the case of so spontaneous and violent a nature as Richard Wagner's. Instructive as it was to have heard this remark, it would be quite wrong to look upon it as typical of Richard Wagner's ordinary mood, or as that of genius with regard to its own works. With a few exceptions, traceable in my opinion to chronic melancholia, genius is happy in its work, and has, quite rightly, a consciousness of success for which Richard Wagner himself, and also Beethoven, often found words. Of such a kind were Beethoven's remarks about the *Missa Solemnis* which petty and superficial critics declared to be overwhelming presumption, when in truth they were no more than the naïveté of genius. Wagner's predominant state of mind in those days was one of profound satisfaction, and such remarks as the one I have quoted only prove that the exalted mood in which he was did not lessen that power of self-criticism which impels one ever to strive for higher and better things.

An episode, unimportant in itself, brought me nearer to Wagner. At the close of the first performance of the *Ring*, a banquet was held in some rooms attached to the theatre, at which this great event was to be officially celebrated and the triumph sealed. A brilliant company filled the rooms on this occasion. One might say that the intellectual élite of Germany had come together there, not to mention distinguished foreigners. The *Oberbürgermeister* of Berlin, Dr. Forckenbeck, who was also a leading member of the Reichstag, was chosen to deliver the principal speech. I sat with Mihálovich and some other friends in a very unpretentious place, swallowed up among the great company. I was a very young man then, just beginning my career, one of those of whom it is said that they "have a very promising future." With keen attention I followed Forckenbeck's words, and I shared the general disappointment which they caused. The famous speaker was not in good form, nor did the subject appear to suit him. His speech was a string of rather banal eulogies, interspersed with critical allusions, but lacking all trace of warmth or enthusiasm. Its effect was to depress the spirits of the company like an evil spell. Two ladies thereupon came over to me; Countess Maria Dönhoff—afterwards wife of the Chancellor, Prince Bülow,—was one of them, the other being Frau von Schleinitz, who later married the Austro-Hungarian ambassador, Count Wolkenstein. Both of them belonged to the Liszt-Wagner circle, and had done a great deal to make the Bayreuth undertaking possible. They begged me to save the situation by making a speech. They had both heard me speaking at a Liszt festival in Budapest, and it seemed that they had been favourably impressed.—I stoutly resisted their entreaties. Had I been asked in the morning to speak at the Festival banquet, it would have been a great honour for me, and I would have accepted joyfully. To address such a gathering, and on such a topic, quite extempore, seemed a presumption of which I did not wish to be guilty. Success, moreover, was highly doubtful, and the situation would not be improved if a second failure were to follow the first. These perfectly sound arguments, which I should put forward to-day in the same circumstances, did not satisfy the two ladies. They were insistent about their request, and endeavoured with all their charm and authority to persuade me. In the end, I made them the following proposal:—"Give me a moment—let us say five minutes—for thought, and when the time is up, look at me. I shall signify my assent if an idea worthy of being spoken here has occurred to me, my refusal, and it will be a final one, if I have thought of nothing."—This the two ladies accepted, and when in five minutes they glanced at me, I gave them a sign of consent. The central theme had, indeed, occurred to me, but for its development I had to rely entirely on inspiration coming while I talked, for at the very moment I gave my assent I was called on to speak.

It was one of the greatest risks I ever took in my public career; but I was fortunate.

The thought which had occurred to me had sprung from Richard Wagner's own work. Him, the Master, and the growth and products of his genius, I compared to Siegfried, the youth who never learned the meaning of fear, who pressed forward undaunted by cliffs and abysses and raging fires to storm the heights whereon Brünnhilde slept her death-like sleep, and who wakened her to life again. Siegfried and Brünnhilde were Wagner and the Tragic Muse; and, in the name of all my fellow-guests, I offered to the Master Brünnhilde's rapturous greeting to Siegfried:—"Hail to thee, victorious light!"—

It is hard to describe the tempest of applause which

burst at the close of my speech from a company from which such gloom had been lifted. Neither before nor after, have I experienced such success as an orator. More important than all for me, however, was that the Master, to whom I had addressed my words, and who had stood opposite to me during my speech as if turned to stone, threw his arms round me with great emotion, and said:— "From now on, there will be no more banalities between us."—I was accepted into the circle of his friends, and a place among them was henceforth mine.

When I recall this episode, I am amazed by the audacity with which I, as an unknown youth, threw myself, in defiance of all wisdom and foresight, into that critical breach. I can only explain it by the exalted mood in which I was, and the impression I wanted to make on the two beautiful ladies, who had put so much confidence in me. However that may be, the memory of this speech lived on in the Bayreuth tradition for many years, as may be seen from the following incident, which happened long afterwards. In the second year of the Great War, when I was already seventy, I was sent to Stockholm on a Red Cross mission. A meeting had been arranged, on neutral soil, between the Red Cross organisations of the German, Austrian and Hungarian forces and that of the Russians, to conclude certain arrangements with regard to the treatment of prisoners of war. The chief German delegate was the future Chancellor, Prince Max von Baden, of whom, I would add in parenthesis, I received a most favourable impression. When I was introduced to him, his first question was:—"Are you the Count Apponyi who made the famous speech at Bayreuth?"—Now the "famous speech at Bayreuth" was exactly forty years old, and in the meantime I had enjoyed a political career which brought me into considerable prominence. But for the German Prince and statesman to whom I was talking, my Bayreuth speech was the only thing that counted. The moral to be drawn from this is that the purely human side of life, including art of all kinds, takes precedence of politics.

I would like to recall one other attractive and, to me, gratifying sequel of that speech. Among the congratulations which I received when I had finished speaking, were those of the great violinist Wilhelmi, who was leading the orchestra in the Festival Theatre. He was not only a great artist, but a jovial and most likeable man.—"You have given me a great treat,"—he said.—"I would like to do the same for you. To-morrow is a holiday. Come to my rooms in the morning, and bring with you anyone you like. Rubinstein, the very talented pianist of the Festival, will also be there, and we will play you anything you ask for."—I naturally took him at his word, and was far from modest in drawing up the programme. Next day, I enjoyed a choice concert in the most congenial society. Wilhelmi gave of his best, with royal generosity, as great artists can only do in private. It was a magnificent reward,

but still greater was my newly-won friendship with one of
the greatest creative spirits ever produced by mankind.

The triple performance of the entire *Ring*, including
necessary breaks, took three weeks. During this time,
there were several receptions at Wahnfried, and I was also
often invited to more private gatherings. Besides this, my
personal contact with some of the performing artists was
very pleasant and instructive. Mihálovich and I stayed on a
few days in Bayreuth after the last performance, in order to
visit the Villa Wahnfried at our leisure with Ferencz Liszt.
One evening remains unforgettable to me. As far as I
remember, beyond Liszt and our two selves, there was no
one except Lenbach, and the painter Shukowszki, who
was at work in the Festival Theatre. With the knowledge
and consent of the absent Master, Frau Cosima read aloud
a preliminary sketch for the libretto of *Parsifal*. The
Master was carrying this work in his mind, and no warning
of the doctors to avoid all mental effort could restrain him
from completing it. We were deeply moved by the
utterly new world of thought which the scenes of *Parsifal*
opened before us. Coming after the *Ring der Nibelungen*
which had been steeped in Schopenhauer's pessimism, this
was a work of genuine Christian feeling, based on the idea
of salvation through triumphant purity. This represented
an unparalleled change, whose depth and significance I only
realised after many years, and not completely until now. I
had to experience Wagner's works many times, and as

often to ponder over them, before the psychology and logic of his progress, and of his whole endeavour impressed themselves on me. This is not yet the place to discuss it. I would only add that the libretto of *Parsifal* was ready a few months after this reading, and I received a copy with the Master's dedication "To his valued friend, Count Apponyi," which I cherish as a priceless gift.

One of the evenings which we spent in this way at the Wahnfried villa led to the only musical experience which I can set beside the rehearsal where Liszt played Beethoven's E Flat Concerto. A few of us were together at Wahnfried after dinner. Wagner, being tired, had left the company, and Ferencz Liszt took the lead in a conversation which turned on Beethoven's last sonatas. Liszt was very interesting on the subject. He spoke especially of the famous *Hammerklavier*, and more particularly of the fine adagio in F Sharp minor which it contains. In the midst of a sentence he stood up and exclaimed:—"I will prove it to you!"—We retired to the music-room, which at Wahnfried reached from ground level, past the first floor and up to the glass roof. On the first floor there is an open gallery, on which the bedroom doors open, and from which a spiral staircase leads down to the ground floor. In the middle of the hall stood the huge piano, at which Liszt sat down, and filled our souls with the mysticism of Beethoven's last works. The atmosphere in which we listened was essentially that of the rehearsal in Budapest, but the absence of any accompaniment, or of any visible *mise en scène*, and the thought that we were in Richard Wagner's house, gave it a character of its own. As on that other occasion, Liszt seemed once more to have surpassed himself, to have established an inexplicable, direct contact with the dead genius whose interpretation for him was a religious task. When the last bars of that mysterious work had died away, we stood silent and motionless. Suddenly, from the gallery on the first floor, there came a tremendous uproar, and Richard Wagner in his nightshirt came thundering, rather than running, down the stairs. He flung his arms round Liszt's neck and, sobbing with emotion, thanked him in broken phrases for the wonderful gift he had received. His bedroom led on to the inner gallery, and he had apparently crept out in silence on hearing the first notes and remained there without giving a sign of his presence. Once more, I witnessed the meeting of those three—Beethoven, the great deceased master, and the two best qualified of all living men to guard his tradition. This experience still lives within me as vividly as the other, and has confirmed and deepened my innermost conviction that those three great men belonged to one another.

Before going on to the first performance of *Parsifal*, I must admit that I did not at once understand that opera. After what has been said, this must seem surprising, and I was myself upset by it at the time. The obstacle to my understanding was soon removed. I discussed it in detail with Ferencz Liszt, who described *Parsifal* as Richard Wagner's masterpiece, on account of its richness both in poetry and music, and its flowing unity. I was not influenced unduly by this elucidation, for I never allow anyone, not even a Ferencz Liszt, to make up my mind for me about my artistic appreciation. Liszt's verdict, however, put me on the right track, and by a great effort of concentration I was able at the second performance to overcome the difficulties which had at first barred the way to my comprehension. From performance to performance, from year to year, right up till the present day, this wonderful work has enchanted me more and more. It would have been all the more painful for me had I failed to understand it, since I feel myself most in sympathy with this work of the Master's from the point of view of my philosophy of life. The change that had taken place in Wagner was most remarkable. I saw him very little at this time, for he withdrew more and more from the society of people who were in no way collaborators in his great work. He was already a very sick man. In *Parsifal* he had used up the last remnant of his strength, and the spirit of that work possessed him utterly. The performers told me that he had become unrecognisable. If anything went wrong during the rehearsals of his other operas, he had always been most inconsiderate and unpleasant, but when *Parsifal* was being rehearsed under his direction, there was not one harsh or disagreeable word, even for mistakes which must have tried his patience sorely. He abounded in kindness and indulgence towards everyone; his nature seemed to have undergone some kind of transfiguration. *Parsifal* had softened all the roughness in him and drawn out the best. I cannot say how deeply I was moved by this information. It affects me no less to-day, when I consider all its implications. It is only now that I see clearly the whole purport of Richard Wagner's mission, the full significance of his life's work, the logical steps by which his development proceeded. Two of the greatest among his works, *Tristan* and *Die Meistersinger*, have an episodical character in that development. It is well known from what incident in his life sprang the mood of Tristan and the opera itself. It is also known how he wrote the wonderful *Meistersinger*, which of all his works is nearest to ordinary human life, as a recreation from the overwhelming mysticism of his last great works. Who can fail to recognise the deep ethical content of these works, the tragic collapse in *Tristan*, and the impressive greatness of soul under the petty bourgeois garb of immortal Hans Sachs? The thread of development leads on from *Tannhäuser* and *Lohengrin* through the *Ring* to *Parsifal*. *Tannhäuser* and *Lohengrin* indicate the high plane of thought in which the young genius found his inspiration. In *Tannhäuser* it is the conflict of pure love with raging sensuality and its final victory—though only in death; in *Lohengrin* the victorious sense of duty in a great mission contrasted with mere earthly happiness. Then follow the years, connected no doubt with the harsh changes of fortune in his external life, in which Wagner was entirely under the influence of Schopenhauer. This philosophical phase corresponds to his creation of the *Nibelungen*. In that work, unbridled pursuit of worldly pleasures, greed, sensuality and, above all, lust for power,—exhaust themselves in their mightiest incarnations and lead to self-destruction. It is the greatest dramatic expression of fatalistic pessimism, embodied in the most tremendous music ever composed, and built on a foundation of wildest passion, yet at the close it sounds a note which heralds a different world. In her lament over Siegfried's corpse, Brünnhilde gives powerful utterance to the disappointment and misery which unrestrained desire arouses, and looks with a seer's eye towards another realm, in which love shall be the guiding force. Without knowing or desiring it, through his overwhelming picture of a world of savage and elemental forces that dispense with any higher law, Wagner had freed his own spirit from servitude to them. In Brünnhilde's final song he shows he had already found the direction in which his mind was urging him. *Parsifal* is the goal he reaches. *Parsifal* completes the philosophy of the *Ring*, and solves the problems raised by it; it is the glorious close of a storm-tossed life, of a ceaseless search of a struggle to attain peace of soul.

In *Parsifal* the solution of the problem is complete and final; it realises what Brünnhilde merely anticipated in her final song, namely, love. Not love, however, in the sense of repulsive modern exaggeration, that one-sided emphasis on sex which is repeated to satiety in every chapter of contemporary literature. No; there is no trace of Freudian doctrines in Richard Wagner. The love of whose existence Brünnhilde is conscious and for which at the close of the *Ring* she longs, is the deeply felt, universal principle of self-sacrifice for others. This principle finds its most perfect and complete expression, freed from every other element, in the love of the Saviour—Jesus Christ. He is the real hero of the Parsifal saga. With this consummation the work of Richard Wagner was over.

Was the Master himself conscious of this development? Did he bring it about of his own intention? I would say "no" to this question. His conscious striving consisted in the unceasing, noble endeavour to reach the best and the highest, an endeavour to which he clung against all diversion, errors and misfortunes. No one meeting Wagner could do other than feel this, however far from sharing his outlook he might be. As for his development, it was natural to the greatest musical genius, unimpeded by obstacles in the path of execution. For music in its highest manifestations is a thing beyond all metaphysics. He who reaches its highest peaks of creation is nearer than any other to that Absolute Highest, to which the sorry wisdom of *ignoramus et ignorabimus* would bar the way for us—thank God, in vain; it is a cheap philosophy which seeks to ward off the world, and counts this starving of the spirit its greatest victory. Surely it is not by accident that the giants of music have ended their creative lives in the same spirit? The lively Mozart,—whose exuberant facility was alien to all pedantic theorising,—composed his *Requiem*, Beethoven his *Missa Solemnis* and Wagner his *Parsifal*. Sebastian Bach, whose whole work was devoted to religious music, need hardly be mentioned. No; it is not a mere chance. It is the product of the logic inherent in music itself, and of that form of genius whose essence is musical. The result is miraculous.

It has been only in recent years, when I had reached a great age, that all these interrelations became clear to me, and when I think them over, I enjoy again, more intensely than before, the great music which I have heard during my lifetime. This is especially the case with Wagner's work, which I conceive as something quite unique, an event standing alone in the history of civilisation. I would almost describe it as the very contrary of that which formed the object of Wagner's greatest veneration, namely, the music of Beethoven. Beethoven was the absolute music incarnate. As a creator, he was happiest where music had no contact with other arts and entered into no alliance with the spoken word, but stood for itself alone, preserving the purity of its crowning significance as the means of expressing the otherwise inexpressible. Wagner, on the other hand, could only bring his full creative powers into play by fusing them with a dramatic text. He has left us no important music without a dramatic basis. If an exception be made of the "Faust Ouverture," a very interesting work, but one which is far from equalling his greatest achievements. If the Ouverture to the *Meistersinger* be cited against this argument, I reply that all the themes in that miracle of orchestral music arise out of the drama. Does this realisation diminish the musical value and significance of Wagner's works? No, it does not. The reason for this is that Wagner did not write his music for some alien text, on which it would hang like a cloak, but was himself a great poet, so that poetic and musical inspiration were born in his mind together, and developed in organic and indivisible unity—a case unique in the cultural history of mankind. It followed, therefore, that all his texts have a profound content, since only this could correspond to the greatest of his music. The poet conditioned the composer, and the composer the poet.

Music has influenced my whole existence, and the fact that I have met some of its greatest figures has immeasurably deepened the effect of their art on my life, dedicated though this has been for the most part to practical tasks. I have been saved by music from becoming shallow, and through it my striving for lofty ends has been encouraged. I thank God, Who gave it me, and the artists by whose help I have been enabled to understand it.

CHAPTER IV

EGYPT SIXTY YEARS AGO AND TO-DAY

As a youth of twenty-three, in the late autumn of 1869, I travelled to Egypt for the opening of the Suez Canal. Only sixty-one years later, in the spring of 1930, was I to see that fairyland again, as an old man of eighty-four. It was impressive to revisit those scenes, for the memory of my first journey was still fresh. I remembered also the world situation which was its background, and the ideas which it awoke in me. But what a change had come over everything in those sixty years! I myself had altered least of all excepting that I would give much to be half as wise and infallible now as I fancied myself then. Generally speaking, my studies had advanced so far that the direction of my thought and with it that of my observation could be regarded as definitely settled in its essentials. Even then, my chief interest in material things, however splendid they might be in themselves, was for their influence on the fate of humanity, from the first moment of their invention until the growth of their total effect. Therefore, I can compare without mental difficulty impressions separated by sixty years, but the difference in the world situation is overwhelming. In my mind's eye, I see three great historical epochs: the first was that of the second French Empire, with its claims to European hegemony, which still existed in the year when the Suez Canal was opened, though its dissolution was already advanced. The second period, which arose out of the collapse of the first in the Franco-German War of 1870–71, was that of the German Empire of the Hohenzollerns, and its predominant influence. The third is the present period, which is characterised by the fall of that Empire, the break-up of the Austro-Hungarian Monarchy, and the tremendous social revolution in Russia. This period has developed out of the World War and the peace treaties, which were drawn up under the influence of war psychosis. As regards my own outlook, the antithesis I have drawn between two world situations explains the contrast between my happy confidence of those days and my present anxiety and sorrow.

The opening of the Suez Canal in 1869 was an exclusively French celebration. I have spoken of the diminishing prestige of the second French Empire, but then it was still holding its own, and the celebration in Egypt was the last glorious flaring up of its star. The building of the Suez Canal was a French idea; England, though she had the greatest interest of all in this matter, stood sceptically aside. The carrying out of this plan was the work of the Frenchman Ferdinand Lesseps. French money had assisted the Khedive's capital in the enterprise, and French influence in Egypt seemed assured. The Empress Eugénie, who had come to represent the Emperor, enchanted everyone by her beauty and graciousness. She was the centre around whom everyone congregated; the Khedive and his entire household lay at her feet. Beside her only the Emperor King Francis Joseph received much attention, for he was the sole monarch of a Great Power who was present at the celebrations. He had come, no doubt, to strengthen the rapprochement with France which had been effected at his meeting with the Emperor Napoleon in Salzburg. Prussia was represented by Crown Prince Friedrich, who afterwards ascended the German throne when at the point of death. He attracted attention mostly as having been one of the victorious army leaders in the war of 1866. The French sun, however, outshone all others.

I made the journey with two Hungarian friends on a Lloyd liner, and our ship was permitted to take part in the first passage of the Canal. Altogether, there were thirty to forty ships, and we had to travel very slowly so as to prevent the Canal banks from being injured through the disturbance of water caused by so many engines. We accordingly had time to think over what we saw, and to sift our impressions. Two things in particular struck me with regard to the Suez Canal: the absence, or at least the moral absence of England, and the destiny of the Egyptian people. There was no need to explain that, of all the Powers, England had the greatest interest in this tremendous shortening of the sea route to India, made possible by the Canal. She could neither remain indifferent to its control, nor renounce the political influence which was necessary to safeguard this route. It did not take long before England set to work in both directions. In 1875, Disraeli's Government bought up the Canal shares of the debt-ridden Khedive Ismail, and by the first decade of the twentieth century England had won universal recognition for her predominant influence in Egypt, thanks to a tenacious political activity which did not shrink from heavy sacrifices. The other subject that occupied my youthful imagination, and still interests me to-day, was the Egyptian people, and the reactions which would be provoked in their future by the monumental achievement we were celebrating.

When the princely magnificence of these celebrations in 1869 unrolled before me; when, after partaking of a sumptuous breakfast at Ismailia,—to quote just one instance—I was given no bill, and my request for it was smilingly answered by: "Oh, Monsieur, son Altesse le Khédive paye tout!"—though I was only one among the countless unknown visitors; when, in fact, I realised the wild extravagance with which everything was done, I found myself wondering, "Who really pays for all this? Who?" It was the poor Egyptian taxpayer, the fellah, purest descendant of the Ancient Egyptians whose inheritance had been for thousands of years exploitation and slavery to serve the covetousness and unbridled arrogance of his masters. This thought never left me, and it also coloured my observations of conditions in Egypt sixty years later.

At a time when economic Liberalism was still supreme I already took a great interest in social conditions. A few years later, as a young member, I was the first to declare in our Hungarian Parliament the necessity of reaching a clear understanding of Socialist doctrines. This I did to the considerable annoyance of the authorities whom this Parliament acknowledged in economic affairs. The social and political effects of foreign influence in Egypt, and especially of English influence, interested me more than anything else. I have tried to follow the progress made in this direction, by means of everything I have read on that subject or have myself been able to observe. That considerable progress has been made cannot be denied. The question is how far the freeing of the masses from the terrible oppression which weighed on them still depends on foreign influence, which earnest efforts are now being made to terminate. Or has this demand for humane government penetrated sufficiently deeply into the native consciousness? In recent years, there have been enlightened Egyptian statesmen who have accepted this principle without reserve. However, it is one of the

cardinal problems of present-day Egypt to know whether
they could carry on during the first stages with a government composed exlusively of native elements, and without
foreign assistance.

On my second journey to Egypt sixty years later, while
in the train between Alexandria and Cairo, I was immediately struck by the difference in the landscape as it was
then, and now. Formerly, you travelled through barren
desert, while to-day you look out of the carriage windows,
to right and left, on to cultivated and irrigated fields, on to
fresh green vegetation and busy workers.

Cairo was unrecognisable. In 1869, it was a large Arab
city, two or three kilometres away from the bank of the
Nile, to which a small European quarter had been added.
It was easier then to carry oneself back into the atmosphere
of Ancient Egypt. The excursion to the Pyramids of
Gizeh, which one is still obliged to make, then led into
the heart of the desert. There was no Nile bridge, and
you crossed the river, together with your beasts of burden
—in this case, excellent little donkeys—and their drivers
in an old-fashioned sailing boat. Once on the further bank,
you left the whole atmosphere of Western civilisation
behind. A ride of an hour, or an hour and a half, across
sand somewhat trodden down by numerous visitors,
brought you to the immense buildings; they stood alone
with the head of the Sphinx before them, inviting the
imagination to re-create their ancient surroundings, or

merely to bring itself into harmony with the magnificent loneliness of these monuments to the Pharaohs. There was atmosphere enough to bring the historical—I would almost say the pre-historical—mood spontaneously into being.

To-day, there are still to be seen in Cairo real Arab figures that look as if they had stepped out from the pages of the Bible, but they get in and out of omnibuses, which run even in the narrow streets of the shrunken Arab quarter. Nowadays, you take a car, or an electric tram, to the Pyramids, travelling first through an elegant villa quarter on the left bank of the Nile, to which several bridges lead, then through well-watered, delicately green, cultivated fields to the foot of the hills on which the Pyramids stand, and where a great modern hotel has arisen, with a pretty garden, afternoon tea, and the inevitable jazz band. The imposing mass of these huge constructions provokes wonder even in these surroundings, but they have no atmosphere, they have become a giant museum piece, whose impressiveness is limited by its material size. I was bitterly disappointed when I recalled my thrill of sixty years earlier; but I was compensated to some extent by the new excavations which have taken place under the Pyramids, and brought to light priestly tombs of monumental grandeur and simplicity. In these there are columns of cubic form, and polished granite beams laid across them; these were chiselled with such scrupulous accuracy that it is impossible to find the minutest crack between two beams, though no use of cement was made. There one sees nothing of the hotel, and hears no din from the jazz band. It is antiquity that one re-lives, if only for an instant.

I did not find the atmosphere of Egyptian antiquity which I was seeking until I reached Luxor and its surroundings, where one is so hemmed in with relics of old Thebes, the heart of the Pharaohs' magnificence, that one only experiences modern life physically, contriving otherwise to forget it. Nevertheless, one does not willingly forgo its comforts, which are all to be met with there.

I never remember having been so strangely moved by a historical monument as I was here by the remains of Egyptian culture. This must be due in part to its complete unfamiliarity. We had nothing in common with it, neither matter nor form. The antiquities of Greece and Rome awaken in us the recollection of a spiritual life which we have largely absorbed into our own, and which in many ways we are only continuing. Are Greek poetry, sculpture, and architecture, Greek and Roman literature and philosophy, Roman law and national institutions, really foreign to us? I do not even refer to the memorials of the Christian era, for these are associated with ideas which are still as vital as when they took on those old forms. The faith of the catacombs lives on unchanged in millions of men. But Ancient Egypt is utterly foreign to us in its content as well as in its form. Neither ethically, nor æsthetically, has Egyptian culture directly influenced us, or only by so much as was absorbed into Greek philosophy and art, and changed out of all recognition in the process. We stare at it in wonder, without the slightest feeling of kinship. Given our thoughts and sensations, we cannot fancy ourselves transplanted into that time and that milieu. If, by long remaining among her memorials, we form at last a lively picture which induces in us the necessary attitude of mind, this picture shows us a completely different type of man, who might be the denizen of another planet. You must dig deeply to come upon the universally human, and even then something of strangeness remains which I would call a disharmony in our attitude to life. This sinister flavour gives a quality of its own to a sojourn among Egyptian antiquities, and marks it as a unique experience. Yet perhaps the effect of other decayed oriental civilisations would be the same. If one comes in such a place upon an inscription or other relic of Greek or Roman culture, as so often happens, one has the feeling of being at home again.

All this does not affect our overwhelming impression of the greatness of a past period that is so strange to us. To begin with, we find engineering achievements, which would arouse wonder even at the present day, carried out thousands of years ago without the help of machines, such as are at our disposal. We ask ourselves how the Egyptian builder three or four thousand years before Christ bored four hundred metres into the candstone rock of the Theban mountains, hewed out of them great masses of stone for the magnificent Tombs of the Kings, then took granite blocks of enormous size from the quarries of Assuan, formed them into beams, polished them, raised them to a height of a hundred metres or more, and there laid them on columns whose construction, apart from its æsthetic aspect, arouses the wonder of experts. From an artistic point of view, what impresses us in the architecture of Ancient Egypt is the wonderful sense of proportion, the power, never surpassed and seldom equalled, of giving an air of greatness and sublimity to pillared halls, whether these are roofed in or open, and to the pylons which stand at the entrance of buildings. The wonderful proportion and surprisingly beautiful form of the pillars themselves are also impressive, with their alternation between papyrus and lotus capitals. The vastness of these giant buildings is shaped to an æsthetic harmony. Their effect is purposeful and well thought out, being the image of an efficient, methodically organised state, under the control of a ruling idea.

This architectural achievement, for which I have an unreserved admiration, has its complement in sculptured works that move me less powerfully. However much I may admire the technical finish of execution in the giant statues, and the pictorial carvings on the pillars and the walls, I am not able to see in them the working of a rich artistic imagination. There are a limited number of subjects which are everlastingly repeated; the king offering incense or flowers to this god or to that, or catching with one hand a group of prisoners by the hair, while the other is raised to strike; the Holy Vessel of the Nile, occasionally the embrace of a Royal bridal pair, and splendid representations of animals. I do not feel competent to judge these, but record only my impression, which was far less powerful in the case of the sculptures, while I gladly bow to the achievements of Ancient Egypt in architecture.

What causes us to be repelled by, and at the same time admire, these great works? The question can only be answered if we probe deeper into the philosophical background of Egyptian culture.

These works are steeped in a faith of the hereafter. Everything serves the idea of man's continuance beyond this present life. Hence their greatest creations are stiff, sometimes conventional, and always highly stylised. There were, no doubt, exceptional artistic works which were free from these prescriptions, and gave expression to the purely human element. From time to time, you come upon an example, as I did in the Cairo museum, where I found a little group of statuettes representing a family in a naïf and delightfully realistic way. Father and mother are sitting on a mound; below it the youngsters, who are vividly represented with their thumbs in their mouths. Such purely human relics, however, are not often to be met with. The dominant motif in Ancient Egyptian art was a divorce from life and a tremendous insistence on the other world. One might imagine that a culture which rests on such a basis would be nearer in spirit to the Christian outlook, founded as this is on beliefs concerning the next life, than is the art of Ancient Greece, which looks no further than its joy in earthly beauty. That it is not so is due to a fundamental difference between the Ancient Egyptian faith in survival and the Christian view. Greek art, which was neutral on this point, seems less remote than the Egyptian, which portrays a conception of the hereafter entirely different from our own. The substance of this Egyptian conception was completely terrestrial. It could not conceive of survival after death except in a bodily form. Hence, the extreme care used in preserving the corpse, and, since even these efforts might fail, the erection of statues to the mighty as a substitute for their bodies. The poor also had little dolls for this purpose, crowds of which are to be seen in the museum. Now, it was thought that the dead man would have to live in the next world according to his earthly rank. Therefore, the tombs of the great were lavishly provided with all the finery and possessions enjoyed in this life. The disagreement, indeed the antithesis between Ancient Egyptian and Christian cults of the hereafter is obvious. For the Christian, all differences between man and man that depend on external conditions will be levelled out in the other world. Moral worth is all that counts, while external circumstances are of no importance, or only in the sense that those who are weary and heavy-laden here find it easier to attain the beatitude of the beyond. This is a conception filled with the spirit of universal love. For the Egyptian, on the other hand, the advantages enjoyed by a great man in this world continue after death. He will still have slaves, command, oppress, and monopolise the good things as he has done on earth. According to their view he will remain as arrogant and hard-hearted in the hereafter as he has been in life. Even the sincerest admirer of that imposing culture finds something repellent in its complete lack of the element of love. Love between individuals there was unquestionably, for we have literary and pictorial proofs of it. Conjugal love, parental love, the love of friends—these are inseparable from human nature. It never happened, though, that love of mankind, and esteem for man as such, was built into that social scheme, still less did it form a part of the foundations. On a basis of moderate wisdom and of a frigid religious cult, the Egyptian raised an edifice of force, oppression and fear, which granted pomp and fame to a few powerful men, but weighed unbearably on the masses, and often degenerated into the most terrible cruelty.

In what did the engineering genius really consist, which achieved such wonderful results with very primitive

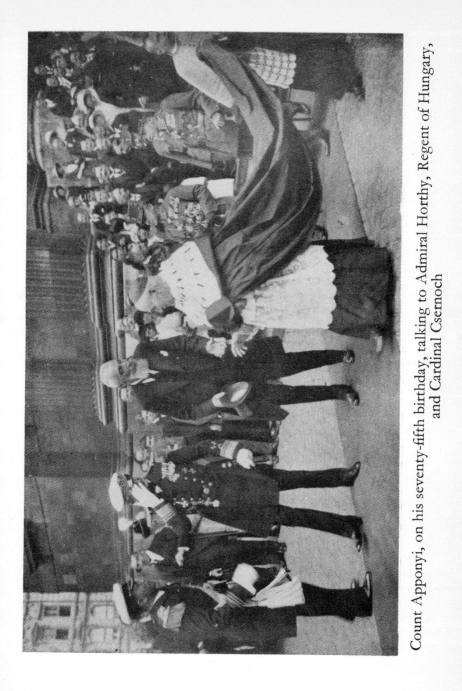

Count Apponyi, on his seventy-fifth birthday, talking to Admiral Horthy, Regent of Hungary, and Cardinal Csernoch

instruments? In a boundless contempt for human life, what did it matter if hundreds of men were killed, and thousands died of overwork, when raising the granite blocks? On the Tombs of the Kings rows of picked workmen laboured in shifts; forbidden to mix with other men, as the secret of the Tomb had to be preserved, once their work was completed they were put to death. At the celebrations after a victory, the King's chariot was driven with stone wheels over the bodies of the prisoners. There was no charitable Rhadames except in *Aïda*. I cannot forget this cruel background of a brilliant culture, and it sneers at me from every pillar in each of its splendid buildings. Considering such facts, does it carry any weight that wise Egyptian sayings can also be quoted in which a higher ethical view of kingship is expressed?

We can have no affinity with any past culture, however brilliant, which does not grasp the notion of humanity. On account of their approach to this idea, we feel attracted by Indian philosophy, and obliged to pay a certain respect to the ancient wisdom of China. In the case of peoples such as the Greeks and Romans, with whom we have a cultural affinity, men were perforce brought near to this conception by the democratic institutions in their own country. Moreover, the philosophy of those peoples has advanced to a notion of justice and a consciousness of the general welfare as the aim of statecraft. Here, already, the Greeks and Romans came so near to the conception of love for mankind that their culture for this very reason is not entirely foreign to us. Universal love for humanity only asserts itself in union with monotheism, to which it is logically, psychologically and historically bound. It first becomes accepted as a basic principle in the Christian teaching, whence it has pervaded the institutions of human society through a slow process of development. This is even now far from being complete, though it still makes progress, thanks to the expansive force of the teaching, and despite all set-backs, such as the secession of large numbers of Christians. I have been led to make these observations by the mingled feelings which those colossal relics of Ancient Egyptian culture awoke in me.

Anyone who spends a few days in Luxor can, with a little imagination, re-create for himself Ancient Thebes; he can even do so more completely than was possible to the Egyptians of the time of the Pharaohs. For our picture to-day includes the gorges of a mountain range which held the tombs of his kings, a thing the Egyptian's profane eye never saw. Modern man can see what was then reserved for the gods and the spirits of the distinguished dead: the artistic decorations, the splendid ornaments, and the whole mystery of these tombs. He has forced open the gates that lead to them, and barbarously proceeded to enrich his museums and his collections with their treasures, —for I cannot express it otherwise—even with mummies, the mortal remains of those who made them. This may be regarded as the Nemesis which overtakes such arrogance, as reached even into the tomb. Hoping to keep its privileges in the hereafter at the expense of human lives, it is thus deprived even of the rest to which every man has a right in the grave. But it is none the less desecration of tombs, and I understand the popular belief which sees in the early death of Tutankhamen's discoverer a secret revenge taken by the dead man against those who disturbed him. There is, by the way, a movement on foot to forbid the removal of mummies from their tombs, and to return those already in museums to their original surroundings. I give this proposal my enthusiastic support, for however little sympathy I have with the idea of self-glorification in the tomb, I believe all the more strongly in the sanctity of a last resting-place, be it four thousand years or twenty-four hours old.

Nevertheless, for the visitor of to-day who wishes to experience the greatness of antiquity, and actually does so, Thebes and the whole district of the Tombs of the Kings and their contents, have become richer and more wonderful. Everything there is in perfect spiritual continuity with the remains of those magnificent buildings, such as the four or five temples on that wide stretch of the Nile's left bank, or the temples of Luxor and the incomparably fine remains of Karnak on the right bank. It is these buildings which, on looking back, provide the landmarks for a mental reconstruction of the plan of Thebes, and the impression it leaves enables us to recall the whole life of that monster city; the sinister doings of the priests of Ammon in the temples, the terrible majesty of the Royal palace standing beside them, so dreaded by the poor, so ridden with intrigues and conspiracies, the bustling life of the streets in which all the races of a populous empire went about their business, the festive processions, and the military parades. In short, a life rich in colour and in form, differing profoundly from our own in everything which does not belong to the very roots of human nature, and of our common being.

I have already said that love, the love of mankind, was a very stunted growth in the social life of Ancient Egypt. Once only a beam of light seems to have illuminated the darkness. Tutankhamen's tomb encourages one to make this assumption. It had been a brief episode just before the short reign of that king, fated to die young; namely, the attempt of Amenhotep IV to break free from the sinister authority of the Ammon priesthood, who were the real rulers of Thebes, to renounce the traditional cult of the gods, now degenerating into mere superstition, and to introduce the worship of a single Sun God. There may well have been a monotheistic ideal hidden behind this symbol. Amenhotep went so far as to leave Thebes with his whole Court and government, founding a new capital at Tel-el-Amarna. Who can explain the motives for this bold enterprise? They had, no doubt, a political background as well, and the undertaking was supported by ambitious people who desired the removal of the priests principally in order to occupy their places. Yet one follows with pleasure the conjectures of a clever Frenchwoman, Madame Tabouis, who has written a historical novel about Tutankhamen. According to her, Amenhotep was chiefly guided by idealistic, philosophico-religious considerations, amounting even to a monotheistic faith, and united with a pure love of mankind which guided his whole administration, as well as his peace-loving—though not very successful—foreign policy. However this may be, his initiative was frustrated by the superior power of the Theban priesthood. On his death, his successor Tutankhamen, though in his heart perhaps agreeing with his father, was obliged to return to Thebes, where he restored the old cult of the gods, in all its pomp and majesty; but he was himself soon borne to that premature grave whose discovery has been a scientific sensation of our time. I am happy to say that this tomb has been treated more reverently than the older ones. The marvellous works of art which it contained have certainly been taken to the Cairo museum, but the sarcophagus has been spared. They have opened it, but the dead man himself lies undisturbed in the beautifully worked covering with its golden portrait of his face, and wall inscriptions on the tomb exhort one to respect the presence of death.

Did this interlude really run the course which I have

indicated, and was it entirely without consequences? I do not know, but I like to think of it as a breath of sun-warmed air wafted into the brilliant, but cold, atmosphere of Theban culture. Together with this episode, I class an actual experience that happened to me in Assuan, and which I will describe here because of their moral affinity. There I visited a few of the plain tombs of ordinary men, which were hewn out of sandstone rock in the hills on the left bank of the Nile during the eleventh dynasty, about 2000 B.C. As I looked at these tombs, I felt a sudden glow of warmth in my heart. There was no pomp, no lavish expenditure, only a fine simplicity in the beautiful form of the tombs, and of the sanctuary at the end of each corridor. These were not places where arrogance reached out to the hereafter, but where dutiful piety and resignation submitted to a higher decree. It was the sign of a more human attitude, and appealed to the eternal man just as directly in his modern form, wakening the sense of communion with a brother dead thousands of years. Here one was directly in touch with the men of that period, with their personal feelings and their own life. The majority of those great Pharaohs' monuments, on the other hand, only strike us as a dark background, built by the victims and tools of a ruthless exploitation, which satisfied the ambition of the powerful, without respecting individual rights, or the personal claim inherent in human nature. Does the act of Amenhotep really mean that a sense of justice had been born in the mind of a humane ruler? Perhaps. One has the impression from these homely graves at Assuan that it lived on in the consciousness of thousands, despite terrible measures of repression, because, in fact, it is undying. All at once, one had drawn near in spirit to the remote ages of Egypt.

Assuan provides an indescribable chaos of varied impressions, dominated immediately by a sense of the power of modern man, which has constructed an unequalled monument in the giant dam, the key to the present irrigation system.

Everyone knows that irrigation has been fundamental to the welfare of Egypt for thousands of years, and that it was precisely this which made it the granary of the Roman Empire. But that irrigation was the work of Nature. It happened spontaneously, being caused by the Nile overflowing in the rainy season, and by its leaving a rich mud deposit over the flooded area when it returned to its natural bed. Under Mahomet Ali, who freed Egypt from Turkish rule, it was proposed to apply the regulating hand of man, instead of trusting to the caprice of Nature, and to turn the periodical floods into a reliable irrigation system. The technical requirements of this great undertaking were only met towards the close of last century. Under European, or more accurately, English control, it was taken in hand in the late 'seventies, at the time of the regulation of Egyptian financial affairs. To-day, though it is not quite completed, and is defective in parts, it has been carried far enough to have multiplied by many times the area under cultivation, and it has caused a complete revolution in Egyptian agriculture, with incalculable consequences for the future. The centre of this immense technical revolution is Assuan, or rather the great dam, which crosses the entire breadth of the Nile for a distance of nearly two kilometres, and lies about five kilometres north of this town. This dam has made it possible always to keep a sufficient supply of water, irrespective of changes in rainfall, in the lake which existed on the right bank of the Nile before the dam was built, but has now been enlarged to a considerable size. At the same time, it drains off such water as is not required for irrigation into the Nile, below the first cataract, where it is necessary for the passage of ships. The dam itself is a dense wall, on which two pairs of rails meet, and it is pierced by a hundred and eighty gates which can be opened or closed. The volume of water flowing through is regulated by opening as many gates as are required. I visited the dam when the water level was low, and therefore only four gates were open, through which the current hurled itself with a roar from the height of an ordinary six-storey house on to the bed of the stream below. A tamed cataract!

If one considers the dam from a picturesque point of view, and compares the striking impression of this controlled water-fall with that of a natural cascade, one yet feels that man's interference with the wild sway of Nature is to be regretted, for it seems almost an æsthetic sin. Yet what importance has that compared to the ideal beauty of this gigantic triumph of the human will over Nature's caprice? Or to its ethical value, since the dam is a blessing, and only a blessing, to millions of men, while no memory of injustice, of cruelty, or arrogance, is attached to it? According to the Biblical narrative of Creation, mankind's destiny is to rule over the forces of Nature. Since the expulsion from Paradise, this could only be achieved in the sweat of toil, and through a mental and moral progress lasting many thousands of years. Even now, such progress is far from being completed, in spite of all the achievements to which we modern men can point with pride. As these thoughts arose in my mind, I returned involuntarily to the recollection of my years at school. I thought of the *Antigone* of Sophocles, which I had read in the original Greek with youthful enthusiasm. I remembered especially the famous chorus about mankind, in which the poet praises the technical advances of his epoch, and thinks himself entitled by reason of them to be proud of his humanity. And yet what relatively insignificant things are those on which he prides himself! That the strength and ability to work of certain animals have been made serviceable by man; that he has invented tools with which he is able to build dwelling-houses; that he is able to work the soil in a way that puts his existence on a firm foundation; that he can cross the seas, catching the wind in his sails so as to make it bear him along, and other inventions of the same sort. Unquestionably the work which brought man to the beginnings of civilised life is in the highest degree worthy of recognition. It was perhaps harder than the later, and more spectacular, developments have proved to be. But what would Sophocles say about the man of to-day, who crosses the sea in floating houses that need give thought to wind or weather; when direct communication by word of mouth is possible between the most distant points of the earth, so that he knows in Europe what has happened the same day in China and can send instructions there within the hour; when he crosses the air in machines which will be the normal means of transport for individual journeys in the future; when man has brought into his service the sinister powers of the atmosphere and of the earth, electricity and radium? The list of discoveries has hardly an ending. If one stands before a work such as the Nile dam and considers all its consequences, how the power of man's brain and labour has won a victory which means happiness and increased well-being for millions, suddenly, amongst all the prosaic engineering constructions that tower over it in a number-less tangle, and all the unmusical clatter and chug of the machines at their work, one is fired by the poetry of the scene. Through all these externals gleams the light of an enormous progress made towards that the fulfilment of that command given us in the Bible, to win a mastery over Nature. This one feels, and yet more—which one cannot express.

The behest to conquer Nature was not given to one man alone, but to the whole of mankind. Some outstanding individual must, indeed, discover the way, take over control, and point the direction, for it is not possible to progress otherwise; but the benefits of the mastery must accrue to all mankind. No single man should be classed with Nature as something to be dominated; the many must not be sacrificed so that a few can enjoy pleasure and power. The great achievement which transfigures this technical miracle—I would call it the ethical poetry of such works—consists in the fact that we have approached nearer to a universal distribution of the benefits of progress. Our advance no longer feeds on the blood and suffering of men, but provides thousands with a livelihood chosen by themselves, while its results serve the poorest no less than the mighty. One is always led back to this thought, for it is impossible, when considering any great work, to forget that man is hidden behind, or stands before it. What have men had to suffer to achieve the work, and to whom does it bring better, happier conditions of life? This is where the great contrast appears between antiquity's vast scientific marvels, as we see them in this country, and the creations of contemporary thought and modern science. When I think what an immense number of nameless and forgotten men were sacrificed to build the great works of the Pharaohs, and then read on a pier of the dam: *"This work was carried out under the rule of such-and-such a Khedive, by this or that British authority, and with the help of skilled Egyptian, Italian, and Greek workmen,"* a feeling of the deepest satisfaction comes over me. These workmen from all countries were neither slaves nor prisoners of war. They were not sacrificed to the work, but came to it of their own free will, being well rewarded for their labour, and immortalised as collaborators on the memorial stone. And if I push this enquiry further, asking whom the dam benefits, the answer is, "Not the ambition of individual rulers, not the pleasure of æsthetic souls in a later period, but the mass of labouring human beings, whose existence it makes more secure, and whose lot it betters." In the light of this idea, the poetry of the dam is far superior, as I see it, to that of the most magnificent buildings of the Pharaohs. I know that much, very much, still remains to be done, even along the lines which my thought has here taken. We are far from having closed the sad chapter of man's exploitation by man which runs through thousands of years, and lurks as a terrible, dark background behind the greatest achievements of the human spirit. At Assuan, I could estimate the enormous progress which has nevertheless been made on this path, and could be proud of the age in which I live, feeling a satisfaction akin to that of the mountaineer who, halting half-way up, glances backwards, and draws from his delight in the stretch already covered, confidence to attain the still distant summit of the mountain.

*　　　*　　　*　　　*

The great past of the Pharaohs, whose monuments affect every visitor to this land so deeply, has not the slightest influence on the thought of the present generation. Egyptian nationalism, which was at the height of its power during my last visit, reaches back only as far as the Arab conquest and the rule of Islam; its character is determined by these influences. A single exception to these limits of nationalism is found in the Copts, the oldest Christian population in the country, descendants of those Egyptians who, after the Arab conquest, and despite all persecution, had remained faithful to the Christian religion. They have never mixed with the Arabian conquerors, on account of the barrier which their faith set between them, and they have therefore preserved the old Egyptian race of the Pharaohs' times almost pure, if we except a moderate Greek and Roman infusion at the time of the Ptolemies and the Roman rule. It is among them that one most often finds the characteristic type of receding skull which predominates in the reliefs and other representations of ancient times. This interesting people accounts for about a million of the nine million inhabitants in modern Egypt. From its ranks comes a considerable part of the intelligentsia, and, now that religious freedom prevails, they are playing no mean part in public life. At the time of my visit, the Ministers of Foreign Affairs and Finance, as well as the President of the Chamber of Deputies, were Copts. Perhaps with a view to strengthening their position, they are particularly keen Nationalists, and would like to make the nation conscious also of the great memories of the Pharaohs. So far they have made little headway with their Mahommedan compatriots, whether of Arab or Turkish origin. Modern Egyptian nationalism is steeped in Islam, and from this point of view Egyptian history begins with the Caliph Omar, and the university he founded.

Present-day Egyptian nationalism is really a revolt against England's predominant influence in the foreign and internal policy of the country. For some time this took the form of an avowed Protectorate, till, in 1922, England and Turkey recognised the sovereignty of Egypt. England reserved the right to keep open her communications with India by a military occupation of the Suez Canal and Cairo, as well as a veto in all questions concerning the rights of foreigners and maintenance of her direct rule in the Sudan. It should be emphasised that the security of the shortest connecting route to India is a question of vital importance for England, while Egypt is here faced with a geo-political necessity which must be reckoned with, however much her striving for complete independence has to be recognised as natural and just. The question can only be solved by a compromise, but a formula for this has not yet been found. The point of view of the Nationalist Government of the Wafd party was that England should be granted all the desired guarantees in the form of a treaty. But it is comprehensible that, particularly after the experience we have had with treaties, that England is not disposed to accept this, but insists on the maintenance of practical guarantees. Even on this point an agreement seems to be possible; the most difficult problem appears to be that of the Sudan, for this offers the greatest source of power to either side. Whoever controls the Sudan, by checking the irrigation arrangements there, can produce at will a disastrous drought in Egypt; hence it is not difficult to see that the Egyptians wish to end this situation, whereas for England it represents a position of unrivalled power.

There is another circumstance to be considered. In the years after the opening of the Suez Canal, during the period of self-government under the Sultan's nominal over-lordship, Egypt's internal position had become so desperate that it seemed imperative for the European Powers interested in the country to intervene. For this purpose, various international systems of control were set up. There was constant friction in their working, especially as a result of the Anglo-French rivalry, till in

1905 the agreement between France and England was concluded. A division of the spheres of influence in North Africa was effected between these two Powers, by which the west was allotted to France and the east to England. From then on, without attempting to lay down any definite rules of the relations between the two peoples, England wielded a decisive influence in the administration of Egypt, and did so to the advantage of the Egyptians. Her distinguished representative, Sir Evelyn Baring, afterwards Lord Cromer, with the modest title of Consul, was the real head of the Egyptian government. Order was brought into the finances, all barbarous customs, such as the notorious forced labour, were gradually banished from public life, and, little by little, a well-ordered administration was set up with native officials. Many Englishmen still remained in certain important positions, such as the Chief of the Cairo police. The complete reorganisation of the irrigation system, which I described in another connection, dates from this time, and it has made possible a systematic agricultural policy. The Egyptian state, whose independence under King Fuad was recognised in 1922, inherited all these advantages and corresponding state machinery. This skilful and well-meaning ruler was able, not only to preserve the inheritance, but to develop it. Meanwhile, the Nationalist movement increased to such an extent that the elections for the Egyptian Parliament, which England had herself required to be set up, gave a decisive majority that very year for the Nationalist Wafd party. From this party, according to the principles of Parliamentary government, King Fuad chose a Cabinet under Nahas Pasha, which was in power during my visit.

This Government contained men of undoubted ability, and was supported by a great national movement, as I had many opportunities of realising. I did so, for example, in Cairo, when the King of the Belgians, who had come to Egypt with his wife on a visit to King Fuad, made his state entry into that town. The ceremony was magnificently organised. Not in vain had King Fuad been Military Attaché in his youth at the Turkish Embassy in Vienna; there he had studied the arrangements of the most elegant Court in Europe, and had taken its style back to his own household. Wonderful teams of horses drew their Majesties and their retinue through a vast crowd. The people were well disciplined and obeyed the instructions of an exemplary police force, welcoming their own King and his distinguished guests with the greatest possible courtesy; but when the Prime Minister, Nahas Pasha, appeared in his car among the King's following, enthusiasm broke all bounds. The real hero of the occasion, Egypt's foremost statesman of that era, drove on surrounded by a cheering multitude.

I had the opportunity of some detailed conversations about the external and internal situation of Egypt with the leading statesmen of the time, and with the representatives of the Powers most concerned. From a general point of view, the internal aspect is perhaps more interesting than questions of foreign policy, whose main principles are easily analysed, even though their solution offers great and almost insuperable difficulties. These problems have not been thrust aside by the fall of the Wafd party, or rather by that of the Government its members established. The crisis which caused the Ministry that I found in power to resign arose out of a disagreement with the King. The origin of this dissension is to be sought, not in complications of foreign policy, but in a conflict as to whether the Crown or an aspiring Parliament should have the upper hand. I afterwards found that the Government formed under the Premiership of Sidky Pasha, a prominent statesman, held as firmly to the conditions of Egyptian independence as the previous Government had done. Its distinguishing quality is that it aims at being a Government of the King, and not of the party which leads in Parliament, much as the present German Cabinet is admittedly controlled by the President of the Reich.

The internal difficulties which it has to contend with are almost the same as those which occupied the Wafd Government. As far as the shortness of my stay permitted, I tried to understand these by the closest application. Chief among them were those arising out of the demand for independence, which was defying all limits. It has been the mingling of European, and especially of English, elements with the middle stratum of the modern Egyptian administration which has enabled the latter to attain its universally high level. "Away with all foreign elements in the Government! Egypt for the Egyptians!" was the latest slogan. No prudent Egyptian statesman with any experience of administrative matters could have a doubt that the sudden withdrawal of foreign officials would lead to a collapse of the whole machine. Even if they were reduced to any considerable extent this would inevitably react on the speed and punctuality with which everyday tasks are carried out, a matter of vital importance to a good administration, and one in which the average Oriental still shows himself incompetent. Pressure in this direction, furthered by ambition, is, and has been, exerted with such strength in every sphere that one cannot prophesy how far King Fuad's energy and instruments of power will succeed in keeping this force within the necessary limits, or at least in restraining its excesses.

As I have said, this lies on the surface. At the heart of the problem is another question of world-wide importance, concerning which Westernised Egypt has become the experimental field. Is Islam capable of serving as the moral foundation of a modern State?

Considered from the point of view of history and of the philosophy of religion, this problem is one of the most interesting of our time. It can best be studied on the spot, and nowhere better than in Egypt, where external conditions have forced it upon the national leaders, who have seriously applied themselves to its solution, instead of simply cutting the Gordian knot in Turkish fashion. The Young Turks have settled the problem by completely abolishing Islam as a State religion. We must wait to see how far the consistent execution of such a complete separation of State authority from its religious basis will succeed. It represents a complete reversion to secular thought, though one must admit that it has involved no persecution of religion. In Egypt the process was not carried so far. Individual faith has been considerably shaken among the intelligent circles of society, but these are in favour of keeping the State in union with Islamic principles and authority. One reason for this is the just conviction that some sort of moral basis is required, another that no substitute for Islam would now be acceptable to the masses in that country. Moreover, it is a political consideration that it might have incalculable advantages for Egypt to occupy the place of chief Power in Islam, vacant through the defection of Turkey. It was often suggested that the King should claim the position of Caliph; but that thoroughly Egyptian patriot and practical statesman, King Fuad, does not seem inclined thus to add to the difficulties of his task.

Be this as it may, the problem exists, and Egypt's best brains are wrestling with it. Its most striking aspects are to be seen in the crisis through which Egypt is now passing in respect to the position and rights of women and in the field of educational policy.

The subordination of women which Islam ordains makes real family life impossible, and gives to the thoughts of men a false turn incompatible with a real cult of freedom, or—what is still worse—with an honourable partnership. This subordination is the real stumbling-block, the insurmountable obstacle to political fusion, in a country under the colonial rule of Christian Powers, where efforts are being made to attain that end. A year ago, when on a visit to Tripoli, Tunis and Algiers, I was able to observe this with my own eyes. In Egypt, a Moslem State with an almost exclusively Mahommedan population, it is not a question of fusing different racial elements, but of reconciling an entire people to the conditions of modern social and political life.

It is interesting to see how the problem of the position of women is gradually being settled in practice, as it were spontaneously, and without definite rulings. Amongst the intelligentsia, women are slowly coming to be accepted as the equals of men, though no general decision or principle has been declared on the strength of it. There are countless shades of opinion which appear to arise out of the private views of individuals. Once, at a luncheon party, I was sitting next to a very beautiful woman, whose name I had, of course, not understood when we were first introduced.

By her manners, I took her for a European, especially as her skin was completely fair, and, as it happened, I afterwards found out that she was of Circassian origin. In conversation, she behaved like a Frenchwoman of considerable culture and faultless manners. Afterwards I met her husband, a high Egyptian official, and I discovered that she was, in fact, an Egyptian and a Mahommedan. There are many such cases. Certain high-born Egyptian ladies who are interested in politics allow visits from gentlemen, if they consider it to be in the interest of the cause they support. The outstanding example of this kind of emancipation which I met with was the widow of Zaghlul Pasha, the great leader and first organiser of the movement for Egyptian independence. This brilliant woman, who has devoted herself fanatically to the cause of Egyptian freedom, inherited the respect which her husband had enjoyed among all members of his party. Her house is a centre for political meetings, and a part of it is kept expressly for that purpose. I was honoured by being counted as a guest of this category.

Accompanied by my wife, I accepted her invitation and spent an hour and a half or two hours at her house, during which she gave us the most interesting account of her husband's plans, disappointments, sufferings, and final triumph. After having been imprisoned for some time by the English, Zaghlul Pasha had become the first constitutional Minister under King Fuad, who still cherishes a great admiration for him. She told her narrative in purest French, and through it shone her ardour and fanatical faith in the ideals whose prophetess this remarkable woman has become to her political friends. She has an imposing presence and a self-possession which belong only to those who are distinguished by nature. One could not leave her without being deeply impressed. The seriousness of the Egyptian national movement was brought nearer to a foreigner's understanding by her explanations.

If we descend to lower social strata, we find proofs that the emancipation of women is beginning wherever some degree of European teaching has penetrated. For example, we had a young guide in Luxor who had been in Europe, spoke several European languages fluently, including German, and had been educated at Franciscan schools, to which, though a strictly orthodox Moslem, he remained touchingly faithful. This man owned a house of which he was very proud, and he insisted on our going to visit him and his family. We did so gladly, for it gave us a chance to see the home life of the lower middle class. As we stepped into the house, our guide's lovely wife received us in a completely natural way, and without displaying the least shyness, exactly like any European housewife would have done in the same station. The relationship between man and wife seemed to be quite the same as we are accustomed to. Our young guide had built up an original point of view by blending the impressions which he constantly received from the monuments to the glory of the Pharaohs with the instruction he had obtained at the Franciscan schools and with the teachings of his Mahommedan faith. He looked with horror upon the religious ideas of Ancient Egypt, on the idols and the pomp which required human sacrifices. As a contrast, he dwelt with satisfaction on the superiority of "our" religious beliefs, founded on love; for he regarded Christianity, Judaism, and Islam, in short all monotheistic religions, as a single moral unity. The fact is that such views are fairly widespread among people of an education equal to our guide's.

This is connected with another aspect of the Islamic problem that I intend to examine closely. Let us return to the problem of women, and consider the opposite side of the picture that has been drawn in my preceding observations.

The leading Egyptian, King Fuad, tried, in spite of his completely European education, to embody in himself the qualities, the feelings, and the tendencies of his people, in order to acquire the highest possible qualifications to be their ruler. The external position of women in his house follows the strictly Mahommedan custom. The Queen, who herself enjoyed a completely European education, is shut away from everyone except her own household. She receives no men in audience, and even the King of the Belgians was not admitted to her presence when he visited Cairo. Foreign ladies are accustomed to wait upon her, and my wife paid her two calls, finding a woman of completely European culture and manners. It is evident that this clinging to the externals of the Mahommedan woman's lot does not correspond to the private opinions and convictions which these high personages hold, but to the King's sense of public necessity. The overwhelming majority of his people demand this conservatism of him, and would take its abandonment so much amiss that his throne might be threatened as a result. Among the masses, according to the most competent observer, the Moslem outlook still prevails even in its worse excesses. The inferior position of women was described to me as being one of these by Moslem persons in authority. They told me that it had been unknown in the time of the Prophet and throughout the Arab predominance, being introduced into Islam through Turkish influence. This may, or may not, be accurate as religious history; I do not profess to know. A more certain fact is that the change in the position of women, rendered necessary by modern civilisation, is only proceeding very slowly and unsystematically. Like all other changes in the higher circles and in the national life, it is not yet safe from a possible relapse into Mahommedan fanaticism among the masses. I asked a distinguished Copt if he and his co-religionists, in spite of the complete freedom they enjoy to-day, did not occasionally fear such a relapse. He answered me with a mere shrug of the shoulders. This

leads us to another, and still deeper, aspect of the problem
as to how a final compromise may be reached between
Islam and the ethical requirements of a modern State: the
particular problem of State schools and of education.

One of the most notable Egyptian statesmen, perhaps
the most distinguished with whom I had the privilege of
talking, was the former Minister of Education, Ali
Chamil Pasha. He had prepared a complete fifteen-year
programme of educational policy, which was on the highest
cultural level, and yet of a most practical kind. He
started from the principle of the State school, and wished
to begin by setting up thirty institutions for the training of
teachers; this was perfectly logical, as the preparation of
the necessary teachers is the first thing to be done. In
some places, State schools of this kind are already in
existence, and are proving their value, but their number is
proportionately too small to have any noticeable effect on
the cultural level of the nation. In his plans for higher
education, Chamil Pasha came up against the Islamic
problem, and was unable to grapple with it. He was
planning a State University on the European model,
which has perhaps already been realised. His idea was to
include in it, as a theological Faculty, the thousand-year-
old College founded in Cairo by Caliph Omar. This plan
roused such bitter opposition in the ruling circles of Islam
that he had to drop his project for the time being. I doubt
that it will ever be revived. I have visited the so-called

University of Omar, and there I received an extraordinary impression; it was such as might drive almost to despair anyone wishing to believe in the possibility of raising the cultural level of the Egyptian people. The teaching in this so-called University is imparted exactly as in the time of the Caliph who burnt the great library at Alexandria, with all its accumulated scientific treasures; his motive was that the books and manuscripts either contained what was in the Koran, and were therefore superfluous, or something different, in which case they were harmful. This motto serves as a foundation for Omar's University to-day. The building contains many great halls without any furniture, in which little groups of students are scattered about, squatting on the floor, while they murmur the Koran in an undertone, and in this way learn it by heart. Elderly men wander from group to group, to see how they are progressing, and to give brief instructions. And thus it must remain, according to the religious authorities. From this school must emerge those who are summoned, like our priests, to direct the religious life of the people, to which they can bring nothing but a spirit of fanatical enmity towards the entire world of ideas outside the Koran.

Chamil Pasha had attacked the problem in the right way. He wanted to form a Mahommedan clerical body which would possess some worldly culture and be free from fanaticism. This he proposed to do by reorganising the old University of Omar, and including it in one where theology would rub shoulders with the profane sciences, and where young theologians would thus obtain an idea of the whole mental life of mankind. For the present, his schemes have been decisively rejected by the circles in whom power rests. Can this be changed? Is it in the very nature of Islam, or is it due merely to the backwardness of its present leaders? Much, if not everything, depends on the answer to this question. I was once discussing problems of the day among a little company of very cultured natives, unconnected with politics, when a young man suddenly broke in who belonged to the highest social circles, though he had no official position. I listened attentively, for words fell from his lips such as one seldom hears an Egyptian speak nowadays. He confessed that, for his part, he was not much interested in Egypt's foreign relationships, which occupied public attention almost exclusively, for they were only of a temporary nature, and were not nourished by the essential life of the people. What chiefly gave him anxiety, and occupied his mind day and night, were internal problems, particularly the development of the soul of his people, the spiritual evolution of the masses just awakening to consciousness and of the intellectuals they were producing. The influence of the latter would be very great, while their spiritual anarchy would threaten untold social and political dangers. It occurred to me that, if I were King of Egypt, I would hand over the government to this man or to Chamil

Pasha, though as a constitutional monarch I would hardly have been able to do so, for these two were the only men whom I heard display such deep insight.

What kind of spiritual tendencies will influence the mass of this Egyptian people, which decides the fate of the country by voting, in spite of its ninety per cent of illiterates, and has shown up to the present time a remarkable independence? At present, the nation is absorbed by the independence movement to such an extent that even the religious question seems thrust on one side. The President of the Chamber of Deputies, a Coptic Christian, told me that he had been elected in an exclusively Mahommedan constituency. In time, problems of internal policy will come to the fore, in the first place of the distribution of landed property. The system of large properties is general now in agriculture. I enquired how the masses who read no newspapers can be moved to support one party or the other. I was told that what is called public opinion is formed by conversations in the coffee houses, where a number of guiding spirits are always to be found, no doubt sent by the parties for this purpose. An influence such as that exercised in our countries by the clergy is here unknown. There are excellent boarding schools run by the French Jesuits and other Orders, in which it is a rule that no religious propaganda should be carried on. We find the same thing in Tunis and Algeria, where the great Cardinal Lavigerie, a worthy heir of the North African Church Fathers who lived in the first centuries of Christianity, left instructions that the Orders of the Pères Blancs and the Sœurs Blanches which he founded should refrain from direct religious propaganda for many years. They were to win hearts by the propaganda of good deeds, and thus overcome hostile fanaticism. Judging by the great popularity which the Fathers and pious Sisters enjoy among the natives, his purpose seems in a fair way to being achieved. The same principles are followed with equal success in Egypt by the heads of schools run by the French Orders and by the Italian elementary schools. Recently, the French have set up lay schools in certain parts of Egypt. In short, although England's political supremacy is acknowledged, French influence holds chief place, and Italian second, in the intellectual life of all classes, whilst English influence amounts almost to nothing.

The great problem of reconciling the intellectual and moral development of the Egyptian people with their political reorganisation remains unsolved, as does the question how far Islam will be capable of providing a solution.

*　　　*　　　*　　　*

My journey took me from Egypt straight to Italy, and I paid a few days' visit to Rome. Though I had not made my arrangements with this intention, I could not have planned them better to give me a chance of fixing and sorting the powerful impressions I had gathered in Egypt, and of blending these with my general outlook. Rome was not new to me; I had only to recall earlier experiences. But how altered, how much greater, it seemed to me with a background of that Egyptian world which I had taken in—to be sure, as a problem only—and which was still uppermost in my mind! Rome is complicated enough in itself. What a vast extent of world history one traverses on the little stretch between the Forum Romanum and St. Peter's! To do justice to the two worlds which are expressed by Rome is to widen thought, but at the same time to burden it. The one is of the past, but not dead, the other has existed for nearly two thousand years, and is confident of the future. Whatever must one feel on coming to this greatest centre of Christendom from a land whose cultural relics go back to the verge of pre-history, bringing, as one does, impressions gathered in the remotest past? He who comes thus from Egypt to Rome bears an enormous burden, but mine became less weary when I saw St. Peter's. The elation with which I saw it from the Forum Romanum was greater on my return from Egypt, in the proportion of thousands to hundreds of years.

I admire and reverence all evidence of man's struggle for light and truth, willingly give all effort its due, have unlimited respect for all honourable convictions as such, and judge harshly only those who are themselves harsh towards their fellow-men. Gladly, too, I acknowledge the law of progress. A faith in logical development has been the corner-stone of my whole political life. The understanding of revolution, which is always an evil, but sometimes a necessary evil, belongs also to this faith. Revolutions are most often a consequence of delayed development. There must be established principles, subject to progress only in the sense that they are better understood and more truly applied, if the framework of human society is not to rock unsupported, and man's whole thought to grope in the inane. With the continual changing of all values there must exist some which are eternal, just as the revolving planetary system requires a fixed solar centre. Since human endeavour can never possess this character, the thought of God is a logical and practical necessity. Now this divine power, this God, centre and being of the Eternal Changeless, must be an objective reality, for if He were only a creation of the human mind, He would be as changeable as all other things pertaining to man. Through their own sin, the majority of mankind went astray from this true God, who had revealed Himself to them in the beginning. For thousands of years, men sought for Him, under all possible and impossible shapes, because they needed Him. They moulded Him according to their own ideas, but as these gods were only the creation of human beings, they vanished with the great civilisations which showed strikingly how mankind was progressing, while they always lacked an eternal moment. Only in lands which had somehow drawn nearer to God,—such as China and India,—did men attain a certain stability; but at the expense of progress, and contact with the progressive atmosphere of the West had a disintegrating effect.

The first manifestation of God was made in its purest form only to the people of Israel. It attained perfection, and the organised form in which it was to be preserved, through Jesus Christ. With Him begins the new world in which recognition of the Divine, of the Eternal in the midst of change received its definite shape, while freedom of progress was given the security without which it over-reaches itself.

St. Peter symbolises for me and for millions the rock on which the most daring fabric can be raised. When I returned from Egypt, and was still in the atmosphere of past centuries and vanished civilisations, I walked once more through a pre-Christian culture, changed by many centuries, but preserved in its richest treasures. Reaching St. Peter's I felt in touch, as nowhere else, with the Eternal-Divine, and, amidst the monuments of a great past, I recognised the proofs of an everlasting present.

The mood evoked in me by the immense contrast between Thebes and St. Peter required still to be completed; this occurred when I travelled from Rome direct to Assisi. In Rome, the impregnable strength of Peter's Rock had towered over me. In Assisi, the element of love came first, for this town gave birth to perhaps the most perfect Christian disciple of past centuries, that Saint Francis whose charm attracts every man of culture, be his faith, or his lack of it, what it may. That strength of Peter's Rock is penetrated by love, and this offers, according to my observation, the directly contrary motive to Ancient Egyptian culture. Looking back on Egypt from Assisi, I saw with compelling clearness the whole splendour of that faith which I have always professed, and I experienced in the evening of my life a fullness, a peace, and an inward satisfaction, such as man not often knows. I recalled a sunset in the desert which I watched at Heluan, one incomparably beautiful evening, which possessed a symbolical meaning for me. May the sun shine on those for whom it is just rising as brightly and with equal warmth!

CHAPTER V

PERSONAL IMPRESSIONS OF AMERICA

IN the course of my life I have been three times to the United States; first in 1904, when the Inter-Parliamentary Union held a meeting there, which coincided with the World Exhibition at St. Louis; then in 1912, while on a lecture tour, to which a learned society known as the "Civic Forum" had invited me; and for the last time in 1924, when a group of American intellectuals had asked me to give lectures on post-war Central Europe. On the first two occasions, I remained between three and four weeks; on the last, I stayed six weeks. Altogether, I have therefore spent thirteen weeks in the United States. It would therefore be an impertinence if I allowed myself to pronounce a comprehensive judgment on that vast and quite unique country. Moreover, this does not take into account the fact that profound changes have occurred in the economic and social conditions of the States which could not be observed in 1924, and which obliged even those who knew pre-war America intimately to alter their views. In my case, I can only put forward personal impressions. These may be of some interest, on account of the nature of my missions, for I was privileged to meet outstanding men, and to observe the leading intellectuals of the country at work and in their homes, which I so often visited as a guest. Several years elapsed between each of my visits to the United States, making it possible for me to notice certain signs of development, often insignificant in themselves, which revealed actual changes in mentality.

That I was able to form interesting acquaintanceships in America was due, no doubt, to my approaching the New World with a distinctly friendly bias, and not with curiosity alone. I had made as complete a study of its Constitution, of its political customs and of the light and shade of its social evolution as every politician who wishes to found his actions on even a roughly scientific basis should do. I found so much in American institutions common to my taste and general outlook, that I was not disposed, like many opponents of democracy, to see with delight and to emphasise above all the drawbacks attached to its political customs and the deficiencies of its social order, obvious though these are even to superficial observers. For me, the good far outweighed the bad. I came to America with this preconceived opinion, and it proved in the main correct. I grant that this is always the way with preconceived opinions. One sees for preference only the things which confirm them, imprinting every relevant fact on the memory, and thus building up a complete vision.

So far as possible one ignores whatever disagrees with him, or at least one regards such facts as exceptions. Taken all in all, a sympathetic bias helps more towards the understanding of a man or a nation than does one founded on antipathy. A bias of this latter kind makes understanding impossible, for, to a certain extent, one must be able to sympathise with the object of one's study, and this I could do in America.

*   *   *   *

My first journey to America, as I remarked at the beginning, was made in connection with the Inter-Parliamentary Union Conference of 1904. This Union is a free association of members of Parliament from all countries, founded to assist the cause of international peace. It was established towards the end of last century by the great pacifists, Frédéric Passy in France and Randal Cremer in England, and it soon possessed groups in every land. I participated in its work almost from the beginning as leader of the Hungarian group. The Inter-Parliamentary Union was responsible for the two Peace Conferences which the Tsar of Russia summoned at The Hague towards the end of the nineteenth century, at which a completely new system was devised for the settlement of international disputes by arbitration. This system was indeed helpless to prevent the outbreak of the Great War, but it nevertheless marked an initiative which attempts have been made to strengthen in the post-war years. Theoretically at least, it has grown considerably through various arbitration and non-aggression pacts. An Inter-Parliamentary group had also been formed in the American Congress, which took an active part in the annual meetings of the Union.

In 1904, I travelled to America via England. At Liverpool, I boarded the 12,000-ton liner *Campania*, of the Cunard line, which was a fast and splendidly appointed ship, though not very large according to present ideas. Her sister ship the *Lusitania* met, as everyone knows, with a disastrous end during the Great War. The voyage was a pleasant one, and throughout the five and a half days which we spent crossing from Liverpool to New York, the sea was almost as smooth as a mirror, and none of the passengers managed to be sea-sick. I am personally immune from this malady, and hardly enjoy anything so much as a sea voyage, or even a glimpse of the sea from the mainland. The company on board was in the best of spirits, and interesting from many points of view. There were many Americans travelling, and these carried on lively discussions about the Presidential elections to be held in the autumn of that year. The re-election of Theodore Roosevelt was absolutely certain, on account of his powerful personality, but his Democrat opponents, who had put up a very worthy, though almost unknown candidate, were by no means willing to lay down their arms. Even among the smallest party of Americans on board the *Campania,* arguments for and against Roosevelt were carried on with some heat. Paradoxical as it may sound, in the eyes of many American electors Roosevelt's strong personality told against him. Anyone who is at all conversant with American conditions will understand this. A fairly important section of American public opinion prefers to see colourless, level-headed men at the White House rather than a striking personality. Roosevelt was naturally a thorn in the flesh to people who were of this persuasion. I tried to hear as much as possible of these controversies, while being naturally most elaborately careful to avoid taking sides. I only allowed myself to remark, now and again, that people in Europe had a very high opinion of Roosevelt. "That may be so," they answered.—"Perhaps Roosevelt suits Europe, but in America we have no use for him."—

A witty New York woman, who was a fanatical supporter of the Democrats, expressed this view as follows: "I can tell you in two words why we don't want Roosevelt. He is too much like Emperor William."

The English M.P., Philip Stanhope, afterwards Lord Weardale, was also on board, as President of the English Inter-Parliamentary group, an office which he later filled for the entire Union. I had just made his acquaintance. In subsequent years, the liking we had felt for one another from the first developed into a close friendship, which survived even the unfortunate antagonisms of the Great

War. He was a man of unshakable convictions, and completely unselfish. During the Boer War, he courageously opposed the political passions then ruling in England, which temporarily cost him his popularity. The above-mentioned Randal Cremer was also among the passengers, a pure idealist, fanatically devoted to the cause of world peace, for which he was prepared to stake everything. Cremer was a poor man, having scarcely enough to live on very simply, and perhaps even meagrely; but, on being awarded the Nobel Peace Prize, a sum which would have meant riches for him, he did not take a penny of it for himself, devoting it all to some peace organisation. In the company of such men, I felt like a common opportunist. Nevertheless, I frequented their society, and seized this chance to initiate myself thoroughly into the doctrines they represented. I hoped, also, to introduce some necessary practical considerations into their idealistic efforts, and I found them more sympathetic than I had expected.

I should like to relate one more little incident on the crossing, because it enabled me quite unexpectedly to hold a kind of rehearsal of the duties which I should have to perform in America. The active share in the Inter-Parliamentary Conference which I was obliged, and glad, to take, as President of a rather ambitious group, was going to compel me often to speak English before a large or small audience. I had never attempted this, and I must admit that I was rather nervous about the success which lay in store for me. It so happened that I was given a chance, while on board the *Campania*, to test my powers as an English orator. During all long voyages in English ships, a collection is organised for seamen's hospitals. This takes place at a tea-party, and is accompanied by musical items whose quantity and quality depend upon the talent which happens to be on board. There are always some of those blonde spinsters who play solos or duets on the piano with unflinching stolidity, and a retired Captain or Major, whose unrestrained baritone voice thunders round the interior of the ship. Only once did I have the good fortune to travel with a real pianist and an excellent singer, and then, of course, the concert took on an entirely different character. Another time, there was not enough musical talent to satisfy even these modest demands, and the passengers were treated to lectures by the staff of the ship, which led to really surprising results. On board the *Campania*, everything was quite normal; there were the phlegmatic blondes and the Captain with a voice. But besides these, another person is active at such performances, namely, the chairman elected from amongst the leading passengers, whose duty it is to introduce the concert with a little speech about the objects of the meeting, and to close it by a speech of thanks to the artists and the more or less generous donors. This office fell upon me, and I therefore made my first attempt at English oratory in a comparatively modest sphere. It succeeded so well that the result of the collection was unusually favourable, and my popularity increased considerably among the passengers.

And so this enjoyable, and in many ways useful, voyage came to an end, after five and a half days. On arriving in New York, I was, of course, impressed by the magnificence of the sky-scrapers seen from a distance; naturally, too, I was struck by the overwhelming sense of novelty which meets one who arrives in America on a first visit. All this has been described such an infinite number of times that it would be a pity to waste another word upon it. Once on land and safely in the Waldorf-Astoria Hotel—then the last word in American hotels, and also in American prices— my first object was to visit our Embassy, so that I might arrange a meeting with Roosevelt before the opening of the Inter-Parliamentary Conference.

The personality of the then President of the United States interested me very deeply. He was known to be a fearless enemy of the corruption which was spreading in the administration of America's great cities. This, and the active manner in which he wielded the power belonging to a President of this great Republic, had aroused the keenest interest in European political circles; I had undertaken the voyage partly in order to make his acquaintance. The then Ambassador of the United States in Vienna, Mr. Bellamy Storer, was one of his most intimate friends, and from him I had received a letter of particular recommendation to the President. Moreover, it so happened that the Austro-

Hungarian Ambassador in America, Ladislaus von Hengel-müller, was an old friend of mine, and on particularly good terms with Roosevelt. Hengelmüller had come to New York to receive the Austrian and Hungarian members of the Inter-Parliamentary Conference, and I was able to discuss the matter with him at once. He immediately wrote to Roosevelt to support Storer's letter, and, three days later, we received an invitation to lunch with the President on his estate, Sagamore Hill, near Oyster Bay, which was about an hour and a half from New York by train.

This visit, which brought such enrichment to my inner life, took place in a country house simply furnished but comfortable and in good taste; it stood on a hill over-looking the sea. We were there received by the owner and his wife with informal kindness. No one was lunching besides ourselves and Alice, Roosevelt's daughter by his first wife. The President had evidently wished to give me the chance of a friendly talk. My first impression of him was of a man of unmistakably strong will and clear-cut thought, and without any trace of pose or mannerism. Mrs. Roosevelt, whom he had married as a widower, was a type of natural distinction, a *grande dame* from head to foot, and quite equal to her position as consort of such a man. She never attempted to gain political influence, but was a real force in the life of a man of such vital temperament and active energy as Roosevelt. She embodied the harmony, the contentment, even the calming influence, which Roosevelt needed, and she used her power in this direction with perfect womanly tact. The most intimate understanding existed between them. Alice seemed in temperament to be very much her father's daughter, a lady who could be certain of winning respect in any circle. Jokingly referred to as Princess Alice, she took a great and, according to American customs, very independent, part in social life. Without being actually beautiful, she was one of those types who can never remain unnoticed, and who possess a fascination for all that is best in men. She afterwards married a Mr. Longworth, who took part in public life, first as Senator, then as President of the House of Representatives. At the time of my last visit to America in 1924, she was already a widow, and when I visited her I was deeply touched to see how she cherished and honoured the memory of my friendly relations with her father.

The luncheon was simple, but exhibited an excellent cuisine; as it happened to be a Friday, no meat was served in deference to the Catholic guests. After luncheon, our little party went into the garden, and the ladies soon left us, though they would not have disturbed our political discussion. This was carried on with the greatest ease. Roosevelt was so well informed concerning all European affairs, including the internal difficulties of the Austro-Hungarian monarchy, that lengthy initial explanations were completely superfluous. He put as many questions to me as I did to him, and it was almost as great a pleasure to listen to him as to have him for a listener. His attention was always fixed on the point under discussion, and he kept closely to the logical thread of my narrative. Never vague or indefinite, he was the most ideal partner imaginable for a conversation. I have had a similar experience only with Mussolini, whose character has many traits in common with Roosevelt's.

In our talk on the American situation, I was particularly impressed by his robust optimism concerning the future of his people, and especially by his power of overcoming the evils in their social and political life, which he did not for a moment deny. Strict as he was concerning purity in public life, greatly as he admired honest dealing in politics, he insisted almost as much on efficiency and the power to get things done. "Purity and efficiency" was indeed his maxim, while morality combined with shoddiness provoked his unfeigned contempt. He was sympathetic towards what I had to tell him about Hungary's national aspirations within the Austro-Hungarian monarchy. It pleased him especially to hear that, in my opinion, these desires were compatible with the existence of that monarchy, a point on which he laid special emphasis. We discussed important questions of foreign policy, such as the threats of war which were already looming over the European horizon like ominous clouds.

Several hours passed in stimulating, and sometimes

profound, conversation. When, at last, I left him, Roosevelt expressed the wish, which his manner showed to be sincere, that I should visit him again after the Inter-Parliamentary Conference, as he would value the continuance of our friendly relations. I, of course, accepted this invitation, and, before my return to Europe, I partook of another luncheon with him in Washington; Philip Stanhope was, as far as I remember, the only foreign guest besides myself. At this luncheon party, Roosevelt told us some very interesting things about the administration which he proposed to introduce into the Philippine Islands, which had lately come into the possession of America. I was chiefly interested by this talk for the insight which it gave into his methods of government, enabling me to complete the impressions I had obtained of his personality. He was an American through and through, convinced of the superiority of his people as compared with the old races of Europe, and full of reverence for the Constitution and the traditions of his country. Anyone who thinks that he had dictatorial proclivities is completely mistaken. He was always determined to make full use of the power given to him as President by the Constitution, but such power sufficed for him, and in the last resort he had unlimited respect for the will of the people. The American Constitution, which is founded on the validity of popular suffrage, has also provided in a masterly way against any outbreak of caprice or sudden desire for change.

The means by which this national will can express itself on important matters, as, for example, changes in the Constitution, are subject to such complications that a long time must elapse before the change is made. Hence the only desires that can take effect are those which have been deeply pondered, while outbursts of temporary excitement and agitation are powerless. Connected with this is the distinction between the Constitution and the law, and the control exercised by the Supreme Court over its strict maintenance. Here we have a proof of the deep wisdom with which democracy has set up guarantees against the extremes of its own power, knowing that all unlimited authority hides immeasurable dangers, since it does not make allowances for the imperfections of human nature.

The more one sees in Roosevelt a hundred-per-cent American, the more one admires his understanding of the mentality and the mode of life found in other races and continents. He possessed a wide, scientific knowledge of foreign conditions, and I found him astonishingly well-read even in details of Hungarian history, far more so, in fact, than nine-tenths of European statesmen. He was quite upset on one occasion, while we were discussing some events in mediæval Hungary, because he was not clear which King Béla had been concerned.

My next meeting with Theodore Roosevelt took place the year after he had completed his second term as

President. On this occasion he was paying a private visit
to Europe, and honoured me by staying at my country
place in Eberhard, near Pozsony. Extremely interesting
were the impressions he had gathered at the various
Courts of Europe. He gave first place to the recollection
of his meeting with the Emperor, King Francis Joseph.
He told me laconically that no one in Europe had impressed him except this monarch, and he put this in a very
characteristic way:

"I felt that, under no circumstances, would I have said
anything to offend or hurt him," he remarked.

The moral greatness of the Emperor's character impressed him so as to outweigh anything that he might
have been disposed to criticise. I accompanied him from
Eberhard on a two days' visit to Budapest, where I was,
of course, obliged to leave the Government in charge of
his sight-seeing and excursions, as they regarded him as
their guest.

He was received almost like a sovereign in every
European State that he visited, although, as ex-President,
he was merely an American private citizen. He was universally held to be a political factor of whom we had not
yet heard the last. I met him again two years later, when
on a lecture tour in the United States, to which the
"Civic Forum" literary society had invited me.

The other first impressions which I gathered upon
arrival in New York were of a very mixed character. I

Count László Széchényi, until 1933 Hungarian Minister
in Washington, now in London

remember a luncheon given in honour of the Hungarian delegates to the Conference by a compatriot, who owned a small watering-place on the Hudson River, near New York. He had also invited some of his most distinguished American guests, one of whom came with his "flapper" daughter. When we had shaken hands, on being introduced, the father said to his daughter, "Now, my dear, you can say that you have shaken hands with a live Count." Not bad as a sample of American democratic feeling! It was one more proof that "democrat" and "snob" are sometimes next door to one another, even in America.

We returned from this very charming place to New York by special steamer, and, as twilight fell, I related to a little circle of people the following anecdote about our Waldorf-Astoria Hotel. A party of travellers was once set upon by robbers, and their last farthing was taken from them. Every traveller, of course, had his luggage and his pockets thoroughly searched, and in the pocket-book of one of the travellers was found a receipted bill from the Waldorf-Astoria Hotel. As soon as this discovery was announced, the leader of the robbers at once ordered this traveller to be spared any further search, for it was impossible that anyone coming from the Waldorf-Astoria should have a penny left. The anecdote caused such prolonged merriment in one of the listeners that I enquired who he could be, and I was told that he was the manager of the Waldorf-Astoria Hotel! I must hasten to add, as much in my own defence against the charge of extravagance as in gratitude to our hosts, that the members of the Inter-Parliamentary Union were the guests, wherever they stayed, of the United States throughout the Conference.

During the few days which still had to run before the opening of the Conference in St. Louis, I was able to make another valuable acquaintance, in the person of Nicholas Murray Butler, President of Columbia University. This man is one of the most eminent representatives of American culture and—I would add—of idealism; there are far more such men in the United States than European prejudice is disposed to admit. Murray Butler is one of the intellectual leaders of America; in addition he has extensive connections in Europe, possesses a close knowledge of our Continent and is an important link between the two great groups of our culture and civilisation. He has never entered politics, but has been a real power in the intellectual life of his country, uplifting and deepening its thought by the speeches he has made at the beginning of the academic year, and in the essays he has published in the University year-books, which concern all departments of human culture. He was then just beginning his career. His European connections in particular were developed afterwards, and on his visit to Budapest in 1931 he could call me one of his oldest European friends.

The Inter-Parliamentary Conference passed off according to plan, and allowed me to practise my English oratory sufficiently to achieve some popularity as a speaker, which occasionally landed me in difficulties. In America, one must always be prepared to find the toast-master at some formal dinner making use of his authority to call upon one of the guests for a speech, for no one may address the table without his permission. This happened to me after the Conference, while we were making a very interesting tour through the States of Arkansas, Colorado, and Iowa, which introduced us to the natural beauties of the Cordilleras and the almost naïf hospitality of the Near West. Our first stopping-place was Kansas City, where we were taken round the absolutely new streets, and then given a standing lunch in the Stock Exchange. The Mayor of the town welcomed the company in a very kind and charming speech, which he ended with the words: "I call upon Count Apponyi to reply, in the name of the Europeans." —I could never dream that such an honour would be paid me, as the representative of a small nation, in an assembly where all the Great Powers of Europe were represented by distinguished men. It was also obvious that surprise was general and not exactly encouraging. I tried to acquit myself of the task in a way that should appease this unfriendly mood, and I was fortunate enough to discover the necessary formula. I say "fortunate," for it might just as well have happened that I should have thought of nothing.—"I understand why I have been honoured by being asked to reply to the Mayor's speech,"

—I said.—"The map of Europe explains it. I come from one of the most easterly lands represented here. To reach America, I had to travel right across Western Europe, and am therefore the best qualified to have collected on the way the thoughts and feelings of every nation, and to make them all known to our American hosts."—This idea allayed all trace of the rancour which might have grown.

I recall a similar case which happened much later, during my second American journey, in the city of Toronto. This part of Canada was included in the programme of my tour, and I was to deliver a lecture at the University there. Afterwards, the Governor of the province gave a dinner in my honour, in the course of which he casually remarked that he had to open a Canadian Motor Exhibition the same evening. Would I care to take part in it? Of course, I said that I would, and after dinner we all went to the Exhibition. The Governor was received by the committee, and conducted on to the platform, where he was greeted with an outburst of song; thereupon he delivered the opening speech. At the close, he introduced me to the meeting, and invited me to say a few words. It was as if I had fallen from the clouds. What does a cultured European say at a Canadian Motor Exhibition? I had to reach deep down into the sack of commonplaces which wanderers such as I must always carry with them, in order to be prepared for every eventuality; but this was one of the most exacting occasions. I managed somehow, and, from then on, I was ready and prepared for everything of this kind that one has to expect on the other side of the Atlantic.

The tour took the Conference delegates westwards to Denver, a city whose foundations play a most important part in the novels of Bret Harte, at that time a very popular American author. He describes it as a settlement of pioneers in the wilderness, where rovers and adventurers have the upper hand, while robbery and murder are daily events. It was very interesting for me to find this place, which I knew as the centre of adventurous romance in a new-born community, become a great modern city containing (in those days) about 200,000 inhabitants, strikingly well laid-out, and with a large number of fine buildings. There was also a park, and the usual places of amusement; in a word, Denver was a part of everyday civilisation, without any romantic flavour whatever. I came upon a proof of this when we visited the Capitol, the seat of the State administration. There I noticed a very old servant, whom I at once began to question. He was one of those who had actually seen the beginnings of Denver which Bret Harte pictured. I also asked him about his experiences, and if it had really been as the novels described; to which he answered, that it had never been so bad. The number of murders and tavern brawls of which he had knowledge had not been very great. He obviously did not appreciate the change of times, and it almost seemed as if he thought the present day, with its civilisation, rather tedious compared to those old, exciting days. All the same, on our railway journey through the western part of Colorado we could form an idea of the rise and spread of new States in the Union. We would often travel for hours through desolate country, and in many places we saw only the station buildings and the skeleton of a newly-founded town, with its straight roads marked out by posts. Here and there would be a completed house, a church standing on some larger site, especially fenced round, a school building, or a house for the local authorities: everything pointed to the future. To-day, after thirty years, those towns which I saw laid out with posts must have already become flourishing communities, and the waste stretches of those days have no doubt blossomed into life. For us, this glimpse of origins and of development was most interesting as showing the youth of a great people. Immaturity explains its many imperfections, but also a fresh spirit of confidence which met us everywhere.

Looking back, I find the strongest of my impressions of America to have been this sense of youthful freshness, compared to which old Europe appears to be worn out. Europe, of course, has a greater maturity, but this very ripeness seems to promise nothing new, and to have already achieved its best. We must do our utmost to prove this impression false. In those years of my first two visits to America, self-confidence and progress were the watchwords. No one questioned whether the principle was sound.

I saw the American optimism of those days at its liveliest on my return journey, which I made with most of the members of my group on board the Cunarder *Ivernia*, an old and slow, but very comfortable vessel. About thirty American students, winners of the Cecil Rhodes scholarships, were travelling to Europe on the same boat. That great Pan-Anglo-Saxon had bequeathed a fund whose interest was to pay travelling and residential expenses for about thirty of the best students from all American universities to spend a year in Europe. Two-thirds of the year had to be spent in England, and the rest in any other European countries of their choice. His idea was to strengthen the ties of union between both great branches of the Anglo-Saxon race; at the same time, he intended to widen the outlook of an élite of young intellectuals, by giving them breadth of judgment in world affairs, as behoves the leading members of a race predestined to rule. Everyone on board was charmed by these young men. Their high spirits, though never carried beyond the bounds of gentlemanly manners, infected all the passengers, while they were also keen to take any opportunity of widening their knowledge. They made it their object to find out from which passengers they could learn something. For example, they turned to me with a request that I should give them a lecture on the legal character and the fundamental political conditions of the Austro-Hungarian Monarchy. I did this with great pleasure, and had the satisfaction of being asked by my young listeners to give two lectures instead of one. They then singled out a Central Asiatic explorer, who was, of course, an Englishman. He spoke on Tibet in a very interesting way, for the benefit of an eager audience composed of all the passengers. Finally an English M.P. lectured on the Parliamentary procedure of his country. It was a real joy to see the combination of earnest endeavour and harmless good spirits in these young Americans. My optimistic judgment of America's great potentialities was confirmed by this experience, which was a pleasant ending to the impressions I carried away from my first journey to America.

Eight years later, I crossed the Atlantic for the second time. In spite of the short time that I could spend in America, this trip gave me a chance to observe many signs of progress. When I landed in New York in February, 1912, after a very stormy, and for that reason most interesting, crossing—this time on board the Norddeutscher Lloyd liner *Kronprinz Wilhelm*—I had no longer a sense of being in new and unaccustomed surroundings, so thoroughly had I adapted myself to American ideas during my first visit. In the New World, I found myself tied to a set route. The entire plan of my lecture tour, which was to include many University towns and great business centres, had been mapped out by the "Civic Forum," the literary society which had invited me. To begin with, I spent about eight days in New York. The secretary of the "Civic Forum" acted as my impresario with great kindness, but full consciousness of his responsibility; for, in its own interests, the Association wished to introduce me to as wide a circle as possible in this city, thus obtaining a certain amount of publicity in the press. The part which I had to play in this affair was completely new to me, but I can only say that I found it interesting.

My first duty was to call upon the President of the Republic, who was also President of the "Civic Forum." My friend the Ambassador, Hengelmüller, once more presented himself to introduce me to the then President William Taft. Taft was a totally different character from Roosevelt, but, in his way, hardly less remarkable. He was a man of calm, even temperament, a great lawyer, having the mentality which comes from being constantly occupied with legal questions. He was determined to work conscientiously during his term of office, and to keep his country out of unnecessary complications. During the very first conversation I had with him, I realised that no real understanding was possible between him and Roosevelt, although it was at the latter's suggestion that he became President. Soon I discovered that I had judged correctly. Without making comparisons, I should call Taft a remarkable man on his own merits. He, also, was on friendly terms with Hengelmüller, and he treated me with confidence and kindness. Our first conversation was chiefly taken up with legal questions, and, on account of the interest which these had for the President, it lasted much longer than is usually the case with formal audiences. He ended by inviting me repeatedly to call on him again at the end of my lecture tour, and to tell him of my impressions. I made the promise most willingly, for the tone of his invitation showed that it was sincerely meant.

Hengelmüller took it upon himself to introduce me to leading members of the Diplomatic Corps in Washington, among whom I must give first place to the English Ambassador, Mr.—afterwards Lord—Bryce. Him I knew already. As a final preparation for my first journey to America, I had studied his famous work, *The American Commonwealth*, and had met him during the Inter-Parliamentary Conference in London in 1907. He was then a member of Sir Henry Campbell-Bannerman's Liberal Cabinet. When I met him, our conversation turned to his book on America, which is recognised as the standard work on the subject. I remarked that in that book he had shown a universal knowledge of all the constitutions of civilised nations, for he always explained his statements about American constitutional problems by analogies and differences in other lands; and that there was only one constitution which he never referred to, though it had remarkable characteristics—namely, the Hungarian. He at once admitted that this was a gap in his knowledge which he would be glad to fill, since he had heard that our Constitution existed, and had qualities of its own. One word led to another, and we arranged a luncheon, followed by a long conversation, or rather a tutorial on Hungarian constitutional history which I gave my distinguished listener. It inspired him with a wish to find out more about the subject. Bryce remembered this meeting, and wrote to me, before I was able to call on him, saying that he welcomed me with pleasure to America, and was at my disposal wherever he could be of assistance. This offer was of great practical value, in view of the immense respect in which he was held in America.

On my American tour I therefore had the assistance of two Ambassadors, that of our own country and that of England. I also became friendly with Jusserand, the equally influential French Ambassador, while with the German, Count Bernstorff, I got no further than the usual exchange of courtesies. I could not dream what a close friendship was destined to develop between us in post-war years through our common work on the League of Nations.

Interesting, and sometimes important, as these official visits were, my chief wish was to see Roosevelt again, and to continue our exchange of ideas. Before my lecture tour began, I accepted his invitation, and stayed a day and a half at Oyster Bay with him and his family. There I could discuss with him in complete peace his impressions of Europe and his political plans, as well as the contents of my lectures.

The latter topic was important to me, for I was anxious to say nothing that would arouse his opposition. My subject was the movement for peace and the means available for promoting it. Nations were still far from the stage of outlawing war as has been done in the Kellogg Pact, and Roosevelt was especially antagonistic to this idea. On the contrary, he supported the opinion, which was shared by most of the sincerest friends of peace, that, while everything must be done to preserve peace and to further the settlement of international disputes by arbitration, there may be disputes which do not allow of such a settlement. Every nation must therefore be ready in such cases to defend its conception of justice and its interests by force. In my lectures, I did not take up the extreme pacifist view, and when Roosevelt had read through the outline I gave him, he made no objections to its contents. I could not quite follow his statements about what he had seen in Europe. Perhaps he himself was not entirely clear on this point. His dislike of Tsarist Russia had not prevented him from mediating peace in the Russo-Japanese War in a sense favourable to Russia. for he acted from the standpoint of higher human interests, Yet this dislike caused him to leave that country out of his European programme, because he saw no possible grounds for a common understanding. He also felt little sympathy for the Empire of the Hohenzollerns, being very much influenced by anti-German feeling in England, which was already guiding her policy in the direction of the Triple Entente. From the point of view of the Triple Alliance, I could not consider Roosevelt's observations as reassuring. On the outbreak of the War, it was at once obvious that my fears were well grounded. I sent an article, in which I defended Austria-Hungary's position, to Roosevelt, with a request that he should publish it in his periodical *Outlook*. He sent me a rather blunt letter, flatly refusing to do as I asked. In this letter, he kept within the bounds imposed by America's neutrality, stating that he believed me to have written in good faith, but he added that many others were defending the opposite opinion in equally good faith. One thing only he remarked with satisfaction—and this was characteristic. He saw from my article that I acknowledged his opinion that there are cases in which a settlement by arbitration is impossible. With this exchange of letters in the first year of the War, my friendship for the man whom I had so liked and admired came to an unfortunate end, for before the War was over his death made it impossible to resume it again. His memory lives in me, not in the spirit of that last dissonance, but in the picture I had formed of him as the strong champion of political honesty, and the embodiment of all that is great and noble in the spirit of America.

Let me say in parenthesis, my article which Roosevelt refused was published in the North American press, through the assistance of men with whom I had been on much less friendly terms, and it was followed by others throughout America's neutrality. Even the *Review* of the University of Toronto, though we were at war with Canada, took articles of mine, through the influence of my friend Professor Mavor, and as an appeal to fair play; but, of course, they published answers to it as well. This procedure was, in the finest sense of the word, thoroughly Anglo-Saxon.

In Oyster Bay, I also observed signs of complications in American politics whose consequences affected the world at large. I saw quite clearly that a gulf had developed between Roosevelt and President Taft, and that Roosevelt had made up his mind not to support the re-election of his successor, but to stand once more as a candidate; this in spite of the strong doubts as to whether his candidature was possible under the Constitution. According to American customary law, founded on precedents established at Washington, a President may not serve more than two terms of office; now Roosevelt had been, in fact, President for almost two such "terms"; but one view was that the first time he took office automatically to replace the murdered President McKinley, under whom he had been Vice-President, and therefore he had only been elected once. In the opinion of many authorities, there was therefore no constitutional reason why he should not stand again, and he would probably have been successful, later on, had he supported Taft's re-election now. As he did not want to wait another four years, and as most of the Republican party sided with Taft, Roosevelt could only put forward his candidature by founding a new party, which he endeavoured to do. The only result was that the Republican party, weakened by his withdrawal, was beaten at the next elections, and the Democratic candidate, Wilson, was returned. Wilson remained President until the end of the Great War, and he impressed, not so much his personality, as his vacillations, on post-war events. He was content to remain passive while peace treaties were being signed which directly contradicted the principles he had laid down during the War. From the wreck of these, all he could save was his cherished idea of the League of Nations, and in this his own people disavowed him. It will not do to make a decisive entry into an international conflict and then to renounce responsibility for the consequences of that action.

When I recall the political mood I found in Oyster Bay, and compare it with subsequent events, I cannot fail to realise that signs were already noticeable in America of an ominous sultriness in the air. During my lecture tour, this feeling became even clearer and more definite. The early part of the tour passed off smoothly, in academic calm. It began in New York itself with a lecture on the

183

Balance of Power in Europe, and its probable effect on the maintenance of peace. I treated the subject optimistically—two years previous to the outbreak of the Great War!—before a numerous and distinguished audience in the great Carnegie Hall. Carnegie himself took the chair. The next day he gave a luncheon party for me in his comparatively modest New York house, whose most striking feature was an organ standing in the entrance-hall. This was played every morning while Carnegie dressed—the only time when he had leisure to hear music, and, of course, he could afford the best. Like most American millionaires, and Rockefeller foremost among them, he was a modest and kind-hearted man, who fully realised the duties attaching to wealth, and responded to them in a most generous fashion. He devoted great sums to the foundation of public libraries, and to subsidising the peace movement, in which he took a passionate interest. The Carnegie Peace Fund still serves as the financial basis of all efforts connected with this movement.

From New York I went to Princeton, Wilson's university, where he had taught for years as Professor of International Constitutional Law, and whose Rector he had become. He had just exchanged his chair for a great political office, having been elected Governor of the State of New Jersey, and had left Princeton two days before my arrival. I therefore could form no personal impression of him, but I tried to understand what this symptom of his political rise meant in the evolution of the American spirit. As far as I know, it was the first case in which a scholarly career had helped a man in politics.

I mention Princeton because the two days of comparative quiet which I spent there, enjoying the unpretentious and warm hospitality of Dean Fine, the deputy President, gave me an immensely beneficial rest after the previous week's feverish hustle; and also because it was there I had my first taste of American University life. It impressed me most favourably both then and afterwards. At every university which I visited in the course of my tour—Harvard, Cornell, the University of Michigan, etc.—I was always the guest of a professor's family or of a students' college. When in a college, I lived the life of the students. I was thus able to obtain an insight into the real life of America's intellectual élite, supplemented by the ideas I obtained as a guest of families in other towns, where clubs or business associations arranged the lectures. The picture I formed is about as different from that of the traditional Yankee whom most Europeans imagine when America is mentioned as is a genuine French middle-class family from the characters out of a *roman des boulevards*. The severe criticisms which French and American authors of social novels bring to bear on the dark aspects of middle-class life in their countries do not prevent one from recognising the good and fundamentally sound things which are happily still to be met with. My journeys in America have enabled me to perceive these, to admit their value and to appreciate them sympathetically.

I found among the students a love of sport comparable to that of the English, a serious striving for individual perfection and a noble attitude to life. These were blended with youthful freshness and *joie de vivre*, which I found very delightful. The same is true of the women's Faculties I visited, such as Smith College at Northampton (State of New York). Here several hundred girl students of university age are assembled under the social guidance of older women; their plan of studies is much the same as that in the philosophical Faculties of European Universities. I was a little taken aback when I received an invitation to speak before this audience on my intricate politico-legal subject, and sought advice from people who had had the necessary experience as to how I should tackle it. They answered—"Don't look upon your audience as young women, but as students, and treat your subject with the same scientific seriousness as if you were speaking to a University audience of men."—As a matter of fact, nowhere have I met with greater attention and keener interest for the dry material which I had to put before my listeners. Here, too, after the lecture there were questions and requests for explanations on specific points, such as I always tried to obtain on my lecture tours. The way in which the questions were formulated gave proof of so much understanding that it seemed to me I had not spoken in vain.

The most interesting, though not the most pleasant, days of my lecture tour were spent in Chicago. There too a distinguished literary club and the University founded by Rockefeller had both invited me to give lectures. Moreover the organisers of a great Washington Festival, which happened to take place while I was there, also invited me to speak in the name of the Europeans. The chief American speaker was to be no less a man than Theodore Roosevelt. All these invitations had reached me during the days which I had spent between New York and Washington, immediately after my arrival. I was therefore considerably surprised to receive a letter from the Washington Festival Committee, shortly before I was due in Chicago, briefly informing me that they had to dispense with my services. No reason was given for their refusal, but its motive was communicated to my agent in confidence. Chicago is—or was then—a centre of Czech and Slovak immigration. A systematic Czech campaign was carried on to make our Slovak emigrants, at least politically, into Czechs, and my experience proves what an acute form this agitation had already assumed. The Czech and Slovak elements, amounting to 400,000 souls, were of great importance in Chicago as regards municipal and national elections. Their leaders had told the organisers of the Washington celebrations straight out that they would

187

smash up the meeting, or ruin it by creating a scandal, if I were allowed to speak. The threat had to be taken seriously, and would no doubt have been put into effect: so I could not blame the organisers for being intimidated by it, and preferring to dispense with my collaboration. A courteous formula was invented to explain my absence from the Washington Festival, but neither I nor the leading members of the "Civic Forum," whose guest I was in America, had any intention of abandoning my visit to Chicago.

The remaining invitations which I had received from Chicago still held good, but the days I spent there proved exciting for all concerned. There were fears regarding my arrival, for word had been received of pending hostile demonstrations by the Czecho-Slovak party, and the chief citizens were anxious not to upset the Czechs, who formed a much stronger contingent at elections than the comparatively small Hungarian colony. By a lucky chance, I arrived on an earlier train than the one by which I was expected. Only my friend Mr. Charles Crane, the famous Orientalist and explorer of China, with whom I stayed, had received news of this last-minute change in my programme. He and a few friends were waiting for me at the station with a look of obvious relief on their faces, and no one else recognised me. He had nevertheless brought two robust detectives with him, who wanted to accompany me everywhere throughout my visit. I declined the next day, because I felt that things were not as bad as we had thought. My Czecho-Slovak friends were obviously satisfied with the victory they had scored by preventing my participation at an American festival, and my lectures were delivered without incident. The élite of American society in Chicago insisted on organising Washington celebrations in a private club, to which Roosevelt came, and at which I was able to deliver my speech on Washington after all.

Towards the end of my stay, an incident took place which is very typical of the terrorism then practised by the Czecho-Slovak group. The little Hungarian colony in Chicago, comprising about thirty thousand people, was anxious to arrange a meeting in my honour. This took place in a great hall which I found crammed with people. I had been previously warned that the gallery was crowded with members of the Hungarian Socialist party, who were not friendly towards me, because I did not then support their radical point of view on the franchise question. As I was speaking, a voice shouted from the gallery—"What about the franchise?"—The policeman who was present wanted to hurry the interrupter out of the hall, but from the platform I asked him not to interfere with the man, for he had only asked me a question, and I was convinced of his honourable intentions. I answered the interruption as well as I could, and there was no further disturbance. When my lecture was over, I had to pass down the hall, and I did so through the cheers of the crowd. Many of the audience followed me into the street and continued their ovation. I had to shake hands with so many people that I could hardly get to my car. So much for the facts. Next day, there was a report in the whole of the Chicago press—as far as I was able to judge—saying that the Hungarian meeting arranged in my honour had degenerated into uproar and wild disorder, and that only the energetic action of the police had been able to preserve my life from the fury of the crowd. I was dumbfounded to read these malevolent lies; but still more so when none of the newspapers, which had published them, would accept the correction at once sent in by my committee and myself. Only on the second or third day did a correction appear, at the request of the Austro-Hungarian Consul, but it was published in an inconspicuous place and could no longer alter the effect of the first report. People connected with the press, to whom I mentioned my surprise at this conduct, which I had never before experienced on the part of responsible newspapers, shrugged their shoulders and said I should not take it too seriously. For better or worse, this recollection has remained as the one unpleasant memory of my lecture tour. On looking back to the hostile reception given me in Chicago, I realise how far the Slav elements, who were working for the fall of the Austro-Hungarian Empire and for the partition of Hungary, had succeeded in their efforts, and to what an extent preparations had been carried on in those quarters for the great conflict which should achieve their aims. This was the time when the famous Pittsburg agreement was made between revolutionary Czech and Slovak leaders, and signed, among others, by Masaryk and Benes. In return for their union with an independent Bohemia, the Slovaks were promised autonomy, for which they have now waited twelve years in vain. I mention the incident in Chicago only because of its association with this agreement, which was not then clear to me.

In Chicago, however, I also received other impressions of quite a different kind. These showed up the best sides of American mentality, and one understood the moral greatness to which this people can rise, what a rich idealism is hidden there, a power with which even the most cynical materialists must reckon. All this struck me in the person of one woman, who was described to me, when we were introduced, as "the greatest citizen of the United States." This was Miss Jane Adams, who had founded a Home for Workers in the heart of the Chicago slums. Born of well-to-do parents, this lady had studied from her earliest youth the problem of social inequalities, and the means of attacking them. Her passion for social justice took no theoretical shape. Miss Adams was not a Socialist in the Marxist sense, and she was not concerned with the rights or wrongs of private property. Her efforts had not as their goal any profound revolution in society. She went to work in a practical spirit that ignored general schemes for reform, concentrating upon every case where she saw the possibility of removing an evil, or of making progress towards the achievement of greater happiness. Together with a group of noble women who held the same opinions, she founded a Home in the poorest quarter of Chicago. This soon developed into a whole colony, with schools for the children, adult schools for young working men and women of all trades, clinics for sick people, expert advice on legal questions and every kind of dispute concerning wages; in fact, everything that can be done in the present constitution of society to strengthen the position of the working classes. Miss Jane Adams and her helpers, among whom I will only mention Miss Abbott, have taken up their residence at the scene of their activities. They live always in that atmosphere, which they seem literally to have purified, since cleanliness and other hygienic conditions are much more noticeable for a considerable distance around their settlement, just as one remarks better manners and more self-respect among the people here, whether grown-ups or children. The ladies themselves can go without danger through the most ill-famed quarters of Chicago. Everyone knows them, and they are even respected by the most degraded individuals. Miss Adams and her companions carry on zealous propaganda for their practical system of social reform. For this purpose, they occasionally visit other towns, and in several places they have founded similar Homes for the care of workers. Miss Jane Adams and Miss Abbott have been to meetings held in Europe with similar objects, and have related their experiences to their European sisters. During the Great War, Miss Adams visited the capitals of all the belligerent States, urging them to make an early peace. She came to Vienna, where Count Czernin was Minister of Foreign Affairs, and laid before him her plan to end the War.—"You will perhaps think I am mad,"—she told the Minister, when she had stated her case.—"On the contrary,"—answered Czernin, —"you are the only sensible person I have met since the War began."—Miss Adams is still untiring at her work, and all who have seen her busy will cherish their vision of the simple greatness of soul which her character embodies.

My journey came to an end with a farewell visit to Washington, and a luncheon to which three of us were invited by the President;—the guests were: Mr. Wickersham, Minister of Justice and one of the greatest lawyers in America; Hengelmüller, the Austro-Hungarian Ambassador, and myself. We spent about three hours in extremely stimulating and, as far as I was concerned, instructive conversation, chiefly about legal matters. I left my host with the best possible impression, sincerely regretting the fact that Roosevelt should be the man who did not do him justice, intending, as he did so decisively, to stand against him at the Presidential elections. Indeed, he brought about Taft's downfall, without himself attaining his end. This leads to the problem of how America would have behaved in the Great War if Taft or Roosevelt had occupied the Presidential Chair. The question cannot, of course, be answered with certainty, but my knowledge of both men leads me to think that Taft would have remained neutral, while Roosevelt would have taken so decisive a stand from the beginning that the outbreak of war would have been avoided.

My return journey on the Norddeutscher Lloyd liner *Prinz Friedrich Wilhelm* took place in stormy weather similar to my experience in the crossing from Europe. This time I was more fortunate, for the storm reached its highest point in the daytime, and, by clinging to two posts in a sheltered spot in the corridor between decks, I could enjoy all the wild grandeur of the scene. It is hard to imagine anything more overwhelming. One moment you are in the trough of the waves, while in front of you lies a mountain of hissing and foaming water. No sooner do you think that you must inevitably go under than you soar again to its topmost peak, then plunge down once more into a yawning abyss, to perceive a new mountain rising before you. One can never weary of watching this spectacle. How I managed to reach my cabin on the reeling boat, and there dress for dinner according to etiquette on board, I do not know. The fact is that I succeeded, and that I afterwards felt the same exultation and joy at this indescribably splendid drama of Nature as I have known after hearing a Beethoven symphony, which is to put it as strongly as I know how.

My third journey to America in 1924, six years after the end of the Great War, was of a very peculiar kind. A number of American intellectuals, university professors, retired diplomats, barristers, captains of industry and others, had come together to encourage in the American public a keener interest in European affairs, and a more accurate knowledge of them. For this purpose, they had invited eminent persons of all professions to give lectures in America, but up to that time they had confined themselves to the countries with which they were allied in the War. They now found that it would be necessary to hear a Central European opinion, but this proved exceptionally difficult, on account of hostile feeling which was still prevalent. A German would not have been well received. The former Bavarian Prime Minister, Count Lerchenfeld, had visited the United States the previous year, and, outside German immigrant circles, had met with a reception which was tolerably courteous, but reserved and icy. He told me this himself, when I sought his advice before my journey. A German was therefore not suitable, but a Hungarian was, even then, no longer exposed to such psychological objections. As a result of the many connections I had made during the journeys to America I have already described, the memory of which had not been dimmed by the World War, it was decided to invite me for a lecture tour as the representative of Central Europe. I gladly accepted the invitation, especially as it included the guarantee of a free passage for myself and my daughter Mária. I was then only seventy-eight years old. This seems quite young to me now, as I undoubtedly thought it then, but my family would not allow me to go alone. It was also an interesting opportunity for my daughter to see America under conditions which promised to give her a real insight into American life. She was intellectually quite capable of being a real help to me. We set out cheerfully, towards the end of September, on a voyage which gave every hope of being exceptionally interesting. Since I had been invited as the representative of Central Europe, and wished as far as possible to satisfy this demand, I stayed for a few days in Berlin and Munich, so as to obtain accurate information about the position in Germany, and the views of her rulers. Thus equipped for my task, I boarded the splendidly appointed Cunarder *Aquitania* at Cherbourg. This is not one of the greatest liners, but, all the same, her 47,000 tons make quite a tolerable figure. As regards comfort and comparative stability, the *Aquitania* is undoubtedly one of the finest ships that has ever crossed the Atlantic Ocean. We became very fond of her. The stewardess on our deck,

Mrs. Mahony, an Irishwoman and the widow of a naval officer, looked after my daughter, who was not immune from sea-sickness, with such charming, motherly care that we arranged to travel back on the *Aquitania* and on the same deck. There were no storms on either journey, but for several days the sea was choppy enough to put all but excellent sailors to the test. The passengers were not of any great interest, apart from an excellent Russian lady pianist and a troupe of French variety actors, who gave us a fine concert and an amusing theatrical performance on calm days. This was very welcome, in place of the conventional efforts of English spinsters and the singing of retired military officers.

I was extremely anxious to see what kind of reception awaited us in America, and especially how my old friends would behave towards me. At the same time, I wondered with certain misgivings how I should adopt the tone which would be suitable for an ex-enemy speaking about subjects all more or less connected with the War. I had made up my mind not to apologise for our existence, but rather to hold my head high, while avoiding everything which might be looked upon as provocative. It must be remembered that hardly four years had passed since the end of the War. The Americans, and still more, as I had occasion to see, the Canadians, were intoxicated by victory, and showed it in a somewhat naïve manner. My mission was made easier by the fact that during the peace negotiations in Paris, America gradually withdrew from collaboration with her European allies. She did not admit the fatal Treaties of Versailles, Saint-Germain and Trianon, but signed separate treaties with each of the Central Powers, containing none of the clauses which made the former treaties so hateful to us. It was therefore possible to discuss these treaties without in any way hurting American susceptibilities. I arranged the contents of my lectures accordingly. A considerable part of these was devoted to German reparations, then a particularly acute problem, and I also wished to use every possible device by which the Treaty of Trianon might get an important place in the interest of the public. This purpose could only be achieved by giving lectures on Central Europe, for which widespread curiosity existed. Had I come to speak only about Hungary, I would have met with about as much interest as a South American would find in Europe if he announced his intention of lecturing on Nicaragua, or even Uruguay. I found an English formula in the words, "My subject is Central Europe, my object is Hungary." I was nevertheless resolved to carry out loyally my moral obligations to our German allies.

The committee of eminent men which had invited me to America was naturally not behindhand in advertising my lectures. A suitable reception had to be included in the programme. The pilot's boat that came out three or four sea miles from New York to meet us brought a whole freight-load of journalists and photographers to the *Aquitania*. They created an absolute uproar on board the great ship, which was so crowded with passengers that not one single berth was unoccupied. Another boat-load, this time of Hungarians, came out to greet me before we sailed into the harbour. My arrival was by no means a quiet one, but the idea of quiet is foreign to the true American. When you are threatened with a programme that takes your breath away, and you dare to plead for mercy by claiming a little rest, they say: "Rest? you will have time enough for that when you are in the grave."—This American attitude was already familiar to me, and I had learnt to adapt myself to it. There one seems to live in oxygen. I could never have done in Europe what seemed perfectly natural in America. For instance, on this last journey I delivered thirty speeches in six weeks, twenty of these being actual lectures which lasted anything from twenty minutes to an hour and a half, according to the nature of the subject, my own inclinations, and those which I sensed in my audience. The dramatic element had never been so obvious during my earlier lecture tours nor the contact with my listeners so vital as during these six weeks, which included the whole of October and the first half of November.

This heightened vitality, this more violently pulsating atmosphere, was the only sign of a change in mood brought about by the War. So far as I was personally

concerned, I was received with the same warm-heartedness
as on my earlier visits. My old friends welcomed me with a
joy in our re-union that was very comforting, and the
official circles showed me every attention I could wish for.
I owe the latter advantage largely to the position which
our Minister, Count László Széchenyi, had won in American society and in the political world. Through his
marriage with Gladys Vanderbilt, he belonged to the
best American society, which hardly looked upon him as a
foreigner. His natural tact and a remarkable political
sense which was one of his gifts—and which he was
continually working to develop—though he had never
intended himself for a political career, assured him a
prominent place among the Diplomatic Corps in Washington. According to our arrangement, he did not come
to meet me in New York. My journey and lecture tour
were not to be given anything like an official character.
As far as we required such assistance from our own
country, we were very well provided for by our most
able Consul, Winter, who is highly thought of in New
York. I found myself with helpers on every side and
surrounded by friends, as if nothing had happened.

There was one man above all, whom I have not yet
mentioned, though my acquaintance with him goes back to
the time of my first voyage to America. I refer to the
great New York barrister Untermyer, a man of outstanding intelligence and, as I experienced for myself, a faithful

friend of my friends. He could be very unpleasant to such of these as were not loyal. During my last stay in America, he came forward in a sensational divorce case to defend the party in whose innocence he believed, for his great wealth allowed him to follow his convictions and tastes in his choice of the cases he would undertake. He treated his work more like a sport, whenever some particularly interesting case came his way. I followed this particular trial with great interest, and once, after reading a cross-examination to which Untermyer had submitted his opponents, I told him that I could hardly imagine a greater misfortune for myself than to be cross-examined by him, for in five minutes he would make anybody look upon himself as a rascal.

Untermyer took the keenest interest in my lecture tour. If I had a day's break, his charming villa on the Hudson near New York was always at my disposal for a holiday. He was invaluable as a guide and counsellor in any difficulties which American social conditions might engender. Together with him, I mention my friend Jósika-Herczeg, because he was a trusted friend of this American. He had lived in America for years, and accompanied me on my lecture tour, himself undertaking all the drudgery attached to it, so that I could concentrate unreservedly on the mental work. Of great help to me also was the fact that my friend Count Sigray and his wife, who was born a Daly, chanced to be in America at the

time of my tour. This enabled me to profit by the Countess
Sigray's many social connections in her own country.
In short, one could hardly imagine an enterprise better
prepared than was this one. Its management was centred
in the Institute of International Education, founded by
Professor Duggan, of Columbia University.

My lecture tour opened with a great dinner given by the
banker Mr. Caldwell, which united the élite of New York's
banking and intellectual worlds, of whom one could
therefore form a decisive first impression. Our host
embodied in himself the difficulties which American
mentality offered to my enterprise. In the absence of
even an approximate knowledge of the facts in Europe, he
judged everything by certain catchwords, in which he
was so entangled that it seemed hardly possible to free him
and others who had the same opinions from their net. He
assisted my undertaking with genuine good-will and even
with warmth, but he always had the phraseology of the
Little Entente on his lips, and was on good terms with the
Hungarian émigrés of the Michael Károlyi period. He
could not understand why they should not attend a dinner
in my honour, since they also were Hungarians. One can
judge his mentality, consisting of a mixture of good-will
and ignorance, by the remark which Mr. Caldwell made to
me on the treaties of peace: "I am very glad that you have
won your freedom from the Austrian yoke, but I am also
glad that the Slovaks have shaken off their Hungarian

yoke." I had to fight, not against ill-will or hostility of any kind, but against this mentality of the average American intellectual, which clothed itself in universal good-will and universal interest. It would have been easier to deal with direct opposition.

This dinner, nevertheless, passed off calmly. Since I was talking to a highly intelligent audience, I tried in my speech to explain the problems I had to treat from a lofty standpoint, and it was obvious that my remarks made a certain impression on the people. I seized the problem of the peace treaties by the horns, and explained their errors from the general standpoint of a just and stable world order. When I had finished, a candid conversation started about what had been said, in the course of which my neighbour, the great banker Lamont, a member of Pierpont Morgan's firm, made the following observation, which I give because it also is characteristic of the ideas current in the best American circles. With reference to negotiations that were contemplated for the purpose of raising a Hungarian loan, Mr. Lamont made the following remarks, which I can quote from memory almost word for word:—"There is a lot in what you say about the peace treaties, but when you come to talk of the loan, put yourself in my place as a banker. If a poor widow from Nebraska comes to me and confidentially asks whether she shall put her modest savings into Hungarian bonds, what shall I tell her? As an honest man, can I advise her to buy securities of a State that is avowedly dissatisfied with its international position, and anxious to change it? Tell me candidly what I, as an honest man, should advise this widow to do."—The question was an artful one. I replied:—"Mr. Lamont, you can immediately advise that widow from Nebraska to buy Hungarian securities, and I will tell you why. The reason is that we declare openly we are not satisfied with the situation made for us by the treaties, and are anxious to change them. If we pretended to be satisfied, you would have to say, 'These men are liars. We must beware of them, and I shall warn my clients against their bonds, for they cannot possibly be satisfied.' Since, now, we come forward openly, and do not wish to put before you anything that is not genuine, and cannot be genuine, we deserve to be treated as honest men and to enjoy confidence." I do not know if my reply convinced Mr. Lamont, for he never had to give advice to the widow from Nebraska about Hungarian securities. No actual negotiations for a loan were then set on foot.

After this opening, I spent a few days in Washington, where I had to call upon the President, Mr. Coolidge. He received me most courteously, but, unlike his predecessors, he would not discuss politics. This was perhaps due to the situation, which caused a somewhat strained atmosphere towards official representatives of the States that four years earlier had been enemies, though in the case of

America and Hungary this had only been theoretical.

It was also partly owing to the President's character, for he was known to open his thoughts only to a few. It was a real pleasure for me to meet ex-President Taft again. He was now Chairman of the Supreme Federal Court, and he welcomed me in a most kindly way. He also attended the lecture I gave at Washington University, during which an amusing incident took place. As one of the most distinguished members of the audience, he was given a seat on the platform from which I spoke, and, after I had started, he noticed an empty chair nearer the speaker, where he thought he could hear better. He tried to sit down in it, but his corpulence made it impossible for him, and, to the accompaniment of a roar of laughter from the whole gathering, he was obliged to give up the attempt and return to his former place. This was the only pleasant touch in my lecture, which was attended by nearly the whole of the Diplomatic Corps, and whose contents could not possibly have pleased the representatives of erstwhile enemies, despite the objectivity which I strove to attain. It was not my business to flatter them, but to inform the American public.

In this direction, also, my stay at Washington proved very fruitful and interesting. Our Minister, Count Széchenyi, who was admirably assisted by the Counsellor of Legation, János Pelényi—married, like himself, to an American, and now envoy to the League of Nations—

enabled me, both at small parties in his house and at a great dinner, attended by influential politicians, including Hoover, who sat next to me, to meet official people, and those who held no official position but had influence in Society. Hoover surprised me by his exact knowledge of European conditions, but it was only when the official people had withdrawn that we began an open conversation, in which I had to answer the questions of leading Congressmen. Nothing could better serve the ends of my journey than the test which I had to pass on this occasion.

My lecture tour took me into the most diverse circles: Universities, Chambers of Commerce, Trades Unions, Men's and Women's Clubs, and other open societies. According to their nature, I always chose for my speeches the particular aspect of my inexhaustible subject, "Central Europe," which would concern whatever activity theirs happened to be. Strangely enough, the driest part of all, namely the reparations problem, was expounded most often to feminine audiences at their express wish. Such were the Women's Club in Buffalo, and the girl students' Faculty of Vasar College, not far from New York. There I had occasion once more to observe the remarkable blending of aspiration and superficiality, which I consider as typical of American mentality as the intermingling of crass materialism with splendid ideals. My daughter went with me to Vasar College. At the dinner which took place before my lecture, I sat at the table of the teaching staff, while my daughter was carried off by the young students. Curiosity about details of European social life was uppermost in the conversations which she carried on with them. These girl students not only listened with keen attention to a speech, lasting more than an hour, on German reparations, and Germany's capacity to pay reparations, but, after the lecture, about thirty of them took me into another conference room. Here they questioned me about details and raised objections, which proved both the knowledge they had of the subject and the care with which they took in what they had heard from me.

In general, it was part of my method to arrange after each lecture a conversation about its substance, and this led to the queerest incidents.

I am not referring to the grotesque questions which were sometimes put to me, for these were due merely to absolute ignorance. I am thinking of serious discussions which sometimes followed my remarks, as, for example, at the University of Evanstone, near Chicago. Here a Professor of Czech nationality made a speech after my lecture on the peace treaties, with the object of refuting my statements, and this gave me the chance of a rejoinder. Nothing could please me more than such an extension of the field of my activities.

The development of my lectures into controversies reached its highest point at a meeting of the New York

Society for Foreign Affairs. This Society contains the pick of intellectuals having the greatest knowledge of the subject which its name indicates. Among them are active and retired diplomats, political writers, professors and barristers, in short, a gathering of these people who are best entitled to speak on political questions. The former Ambassador in England, Mr. Davis, was then President of the Society. A Democrat ex-candidate for the Presidency, he was one of the best brains in America. At the beginning of November, this Society invited me to take part in a discussion on the peace treaties, and I was expressly told that a leading Czech diplomat would also speak. I acknowledged this announcement with great pleasure, but unfortunately it could not be realised, for he excused himself at the last moment. His place as official champion of the peace treaties, in opposition to me, from whom the attack was expected, went to an American, a Professor from Williamstown University, whose name I have forgotten. Following upon my speech, which was, in fact, a sharp criticism of the peace treaties, he carried out his task very well indeed. All the same, his argument amounted to an attempt to prove that under the circumstances nothing better could have been done. In my closing words, I was therefore able to say that defending counsel had pleaded guilty with mitigating circumstances, a statement with which I could partly agree. The other side was also represented by Professor Pupin, of Columbia

University, a Serb by birth, and a most jovial, kind-hearted, and popular man, with whom I was able to discuss the subject in a very friendly way. It was, indeed, a most enjoyable evening, and I was up against opponents who were most able swordsmen.

I have mentioned Evanstone, which is a suburb of Chicago, the villa quarter of smart society, and of such brain-workers as desire a quiet house. I was here honoured by a desire to hear me speak to a wider circle, following upon my lecture at the University. For this purpose, the Methodist Church was selected as being the most capacious hall. I had no objection to this, but great was my astonishment when I arrived there on the afternoon indicated, and was greeted by the tones of the organ as they led me on to the platform. I then had to listen to a hymn, in which the whole company joined, whereupon the clergyman delivered a short speech asking me to give my lecture. The clergyman said that my lecture would be devoted to the cause of peace, and that nothing could be more pleasing to God. The congregation had therefore decided to hear my lecture instead of a sermon at the afternoon service. Never had I dreamt that I would act as preacher in a Methodist Church. However, it was well meant, and I endeavoured to accomplish my task with the greatest possible unction. When it was over, the clergyman said a prayer, in which he implored God to enlighten men, so that they might attain to that height of conscious purpose which I had expressed—in my sermon!!! Truly American, to be sure.

In the play of question and answer which followed my lectures, the mood of the public, and sometimes of an antagonistic section, would come out in various ways. For instance, it so happened after a lecture in which I declared that the victorious nations were in such a powerful position towards the end of the War that they no longer counted on the possibility of a defeat. They were, so to speak, all-powerful, or at least wielded enormous power. I affirmed that a position of this kind was more than the imperfection of human nature can bear. It leads inevitably to the state of mind known as the folly of the Cæsars, in which the power of distinguishing between what is possible in the long run and what is not possible is lost. Nothing just or wise can be achieved by men in that state of mind, which explains the errors of the peace treaties. When I had finished, one of the listeners began to speak, and, apparently thinking that he had caught me out, asked me the question: "Very good, Count; but do you think that the Central Powers, had they been victorious, would have dealt more wisely and justly?"

A whisper passed through the people, as if this question had disposed of me. I replied as follows: "No, I do not think so by any means. On the contrary, I am certain that the Central Powers, had they been in the same situation, would have made the same mistakes. I do not draw my conclusions from the supposed wickedness of one party or of the other, but from the universal laws of human nature."—This statement was greeted with general applause, but such incidents proved that gunpowder was still lying about.

The fact that a part of my tour coincided with one made by Lloyd George gave it a particular appeal. At first, I was put out by this, and looked upon it almost as a disaster for my enterprise, as I could not possibly compete as a sensation with the great English War Premier. As it happened, the gain was greater for me than the loss. Everywhere, the English statesman's lectures contained remarks which served me as the basis for mine. An outstanding case was the speech which he made while I was in Chicago. His first day in this city was the last which I spent there. I had remained only in order to accept the invitation given me by the Chicago Chamber of Commerce to attend the luncheon they were giving in Lloyd George's honour, at which he would make his first speech. I did not know him personally, yet we had met before. He had been present, as a member of the Supreme Allied Council, at the meeting where I delivered a statement of our position to that illustrious company, for I was myself chief Hungarian delegate at the Paris Peace Conference. To the great annoyance of Clemenceau, he had asked me certain questions, the answer to which made it necessary for me to show him a map, which led to further explanations. We had therefore met, and yet we had not met; but, in any case, Lloyd George at once knew who I was when he caught sight of me at the table, and came up with a friendly word of remembrance about our first and only meeting. The handshake we exchanged was greeted with applause by the American gathering, to some extent because it symbolised the reconciliation of war-time enemies. In the speech which Lloyd George made on this occasion he stated how Germany, at one point in the War, would have been able to make peace on the basis of common agreement. This opportunity had been allowed to slip, and the War continued until a situation arose in which—I quote from memory, but can vouch for the fact that these words were used—"a peace on the basis of mutual understanding was out of the question, and one had to be signed on the basis of one-sided dictation which was to the benefit of neither party." This sentence, with its admission by one of the leading men on the other side that the manner in which peace had been made was unfavourable to all concerned, served me as a starting point for all criticisms which I henceforth devoted to their framing of the peace. Apart from the advantages which I derived from it, Lloyd George's manner of speaking gave me great pleasure. I heard him once more, when he delivered his farewell speech at the New York Opera House, and I have seldom met a speaker who united all the gifts of oratory as he did. He had clarity, logic, humour—with an almost naïvely obvious joy in his own jokes—but he also had pathos, and all of them in the right place. Unfortunately, I had no chance of a conversation with him, for his time was probably occupied day and night even more than mine, and he left America before I did.

Another personal experience shows the best side of the American character, while it may be taken as a typical example of their open-heartedness. An influential New York journalist, Mr. Jay Kaufmann, took a keen interest in Hungarian affairs, especially in the material hardships which existed in many parts of the country immediately after the War, and bore particularly heavily on children. By a tremendous display of social work, he arranged for a charity performance of an unusual kind, whose proceeds were to aid sufferers in Hungary, to be held at the Manhattan Opera House—the largest theatre in New York after the Metropolitan Opera. At this performance, all the stars of the New York stage, from tragic heroes and heroines to nigger dancers and jazz bands, gave their services free, each one doing a little scene. Even the attendants and programme-sellers were young members of the theatre, who undertook this duty free of charge. The great actress Jane Eagel, who was prevented by indisposition from collaborating, sent a gift of a thousand dollars instead. The theatre also was given gratis for the performance. There were therefore no expenses, and

Mr. Kaufmann could bring the entire sum, which must have amounted to thirty thousand dollars, to Hungary in person, where he distributed it among various charities, according to his own choice, but largely at my suggestion. I think that any comment would be superfluous.

My lecture tour took me for a short time to Canada. I regret that it was only a short time, for this great awakening land arouses my keen interest and warmest sympathy. I only visited the cities of Toronto and Montreal, and, as a result of my programme being drawn up already, I saw nothing outside the English element, which I regretted all the more as I was on friendly terms with certain leading French people, among whom I will only mention Senator Dandurand. I had met them through the Inter-Parliamentary Union, and our friendship had been continued at the League of Nations.

Once more, during this journey to the United States, I set foot on Canadian soil, but, like the first time, for a few days only. I regretted this very much, and still do so, for it would have been most interesting to make a closer study of the contrast between these two adjoining countries, which is obvious even on short acquaintance. In Toronto, which lies on the frontier and looks exactly like a city in the United States, this is less apparent, for one feels the influence of American customs and mentality; but Montreal is absolutely Canadian, and its streets remind one of a French town. I was able to see how contented both

countries are by the fact that there is no trace of a military
defence system on the frontier between them; no forti-
fications, no troops at the frontier stations, no armed
vessels on the lakes which are common to both countries.
On the other hand, their independence is a jealously
guarded idea, and on the Canadian side there is an alert
watch kept for any movement towards annexation or
absorption which might originate in the United States.
At the time of my second voyage to America and my
first visit to Canada, President Taft and the Canadian
Prime Minister, Laurier, a highly respected man, had
signed a trade agreement between both countries, which
came near to instituting complete Free Trade. Taft was not
a little proud of this result, but in Canada it met with keen
opposition. During the two days which I then spent in
Toronto, hardly anything else was talked of. Laurier's
Ministry actually fell as a result of it, and no similar step
has since been taken.

There is an indescribable atmosphere in Canadian social
life, almost a survival of the manners at Louis XIV's
Court, which one notices especially where the French
element is uppermost. French, as spoken and written in
Canada, has preserved the flavour of the *grand siècle*, which
the first French immigrants brought with them. In the
English-speaking majority, American influences are perceptible, though this English element is the one that
watches most jealously over the country's independence.

These nuances have blended to produce a quite peculiar, and very attractive, social tone, in whose atmosphere I would gladly have lingered.

The reception I met with in Canada was just as hearty and free from all trace of enmity as had been the case in the United States. At the same time, the memory of the War seemed fresher here, for the speaker who introduced my lecture in Toronto was careful to include in his speech of welcome a pæan in honour of the splendid achievements of Canadian troops in the War. Obeying my resolve never to be forced into a position of inferiority, I answered these remarks at the beginning of my speech by fully admitting my Canadian host's justification for this feeling of pride. I claimed that we had an equal right to be proud of the heroism of our own armies, although the fortunes of war had not smiled on them. It is typical of the English character that this reply, far from being resented, met with loud applause. I received another proof of chivalry, which is pleasant to look back upon. During a conversation one evening in Montreal, a man came up to me and introduced himself as General So-and-So. He said that he was delighted to meet a Hungarian, and to tell him what feelings of admiration for the Hungarian troops had been brought back from Italy by the Canadian detachment.—"We expressed what we thought of the Hungarians by saying that it would be an honour and a pleasure to shake hands with such a chivalrous enemy when the War was over."—

Chance brought me in touch with other Canadian military circles, for the President of Montreal University, who took the chair at my lecture, was no less a man than the Commander-in-Chief of the Canadian troops in the Great War. He performed his duties as Chairman in a most friendly way. When a discussion started after my lecture, in which a representative of Czechoslovakia took part somewhat aggressively, he defended my point of view in a short, but impressive speech. In all this there was a shade of difference between the attitude of this audience and of leading men in Canada on the one hand, and those in the United States on the other. A hardly perceptible trace, but one that I thought characteristic of both countries. In Canada, there was obviously a fresher memory of the great struggle, a more perceptible survival of the War mentality, though this went with a chivalrous attitude towards the beaten foe. Behind the good-will which they showed me personally was their esteem for the Hungarian colonists who have settled there. They are numerous only in the province of Saskatchewan, an agricultural district lying rather far north, where they are doing excellent work and are looked upon as first-rate citizens. It was a great satisfaction for me to hear nothing but praise of them on all sides.

With the trip to Canada, my third, and I presume, last, American journey came to an end. The programme had been exhausted, and I had only a farewell speech to make in

New York. In this, I sought to tell my American listeners the impressions which I had received on my return visit to their country, and to express as warmly as possible my admiration and affection for that great people. There was unmistakable cordiality in my last meeting with the American public, and, as I left them, I felt that I had received far more than I had given. I certainly took away rich material for thought and mental study during the calm, placid voyage home on the *Aquitania*.

When I think over the memories of my three American voyages, I perceive, first and foremost, a continually growing regard there for the things of the spirit, whose significance has become greater in the life of the American people. I have remarked already that the election of a celebrated scholar and Professor to be President of the Union marked something quite new in American public life, but I could mention other, less obvious, symptoms which point in the same direction. I could indicate the enormous progress which has been made in the pursuit of certain sciences, particularly in medical science. A deeper understanding of great music was also obvious to me in certain striking ways. For instance, during my visit in 1912, I heard a splendid performance of the *Meistersinger* conducted by Toscanini at the New York Metropolitan Opera House, but I noticed with disagreeable surprise that the public continued to chatter during the wonderful introduction to the third act, because the curtain had not gone up, and they assumed that it was only unimportant music played during the interval. In 1924, when I attended another performance of the *Meistersinger*, there was a devout silence in the theatre during this same introductory music. A detail, if you will, but it shows how public appreciation of what is great in music had grown. On my journeys I was always determined not to wallow in the mud of democratic abuses, notorious and repeatedly mentioned as these are, nor to investigate such evils as the corruption of certain great cities, the excessive power of plutocrats, and similar unfavourable aspects of American life. On the contrary, I tried to acquaint myself with the other, and better, side, namely the æsthetic and moral aspect, of the life of this great nation. I wished to see the idealism ruling in many circles, which has perhaps a more naïf character than in old Europe, but which is a real power of light against the forces of darkness. I learnt that the abuses of the plutocracy have their reverse side in a sense of duty to the people, which has led to the founding of many superb cultural and humanitarian institutions, scattered over the entire Union. I also appreciated more deeply certain monuments to human greatness, and especially the memorials to the two greatest Americans, Washington and Lincoln, which must affect anyone who knows their history. On my last visit to Washington, I was deeply moved by the lessons which are to be derived from Lincoln's tomb there. My farewell speech was inspired chiefly by this theme. The walls of Lincoln's mausoleum are covered with inscriptions taken from his messages to Congress during the Civil War. These quotations have the power of Biblical texts. We read, for example, how Lincoln, on his re-election to the Presidency during the Civil War, sent a message to Congress, regretting the terrible misfortune of this strife between brothers, and ending with the words:—"God's chastisement has afflicted us because of the sin that our forefathers wrought on the innocent negroes, when they brought them here into slavery,"—and then later:—"We must still bear arms against the champions of slavery. It is hard to assume good faith in such adversaries, and in the defenders of such a cause, but yet I say, 'Judge not, that ye be not judged.' "

Such simple human greatness speaks in these and similar quotations, such deep Christian feeling, that one not only stands in admiration and wonder before the memorial of the man who said them, but realises what must lie in the heart of this people, whose chosen leader could speak to them like this at the greatest crisis of their national existence. Lincoln seemed to me, too, the pattern of a victorious peacemaker, and the peace which he made after the Civil War, an example of the way in which peace should be secured. I mean by this that no thorn should remain in the flesh of the vanquished, no incurable wounds, in which lie the germs of a new conflict. When the Northern troops, who were fighting to maintain the

Union, had won a victory which decided the American War of Secession, and President Lincoln could dictate terms of peace, much as the victorious Powers at the end of our World War, there were voices around him claiming that the defeated Southern States—which the victors looked upon as rebels—should be punished for their conduct by being obliged to forfeit their rights. All the passions which had been surging in the victors' hearts through years of bitter struggle demanded such a verdict. Lincoln would have none of it. He decided in favour of a peace which required no more from the defeated Southern States than a return to law and order, and the recognition of the definite, irrevocable abolition of slavery. When General Lee, the brilliant military leader of the defeated Southern States, asked General Ulysses Grant, Commander-in-Chief of the victorious Northern Army, what he should do with the 14,000 horses belonging to his surviving cavalry, Grant said:—"Take them home with you. You will need them for your fields."—

That is how peace is made, when one really wants peace, and when one is full of the spirit of that quotation which I recalled above. What were the consequences? The restoration of the Union, rapid healing of the wounds which the Civil War had made and a return of power and prosperity to the great Republic. A peace of hatred and revenge, such as always commends itself in time of war, and was urged upon Lincoln by the public mood, would

have perpetuated the breach, and in all likelihood might
have brought forth fresh Civil Wars and signified the end
of the power and prosperity of the Union. A democracy
which produces such men, and which makes it possible to
follow such doctrines in moments of wildest passion,
must be filled with great and good impulses. Whoever
will not admit this, or passes by without appreciating it,
has an eye for darkness only, and not for light.

With thoughts and feelings such as these, I left the
America of 1924. Has it any connection, I wonder, with
that of 1932? The America of 1923 was still exactly as in
pre-war days. No lasting change seemed to have occurred,
either in business conditions or in the whole social and
political organism, nor was it apparent in the soul of the
people. The War seemed a passing episode, not the
origin of a profound change in all aspects of life, as we now
see it to have been. There was no trace of such an idea
then. No one talked of the spread of gangsterdom, or of
the kidnapping of children, or of the unreliability of the
police, not to mention the economic collapse, which, after
a dazzling interlude, has broken illusions in America and
all over the world, bringing to light in a terrible way the
consequences of the War. The most recent books about
America—to cite only André Siegfried's monumental
work—give evidence of changes in the political outlook
which were not then to be perceived. I cannot, therefore,
know if the impressions of which I have tried to give an

informal account here still have any significance, except as personal memories, if they contain traits of a reality that still exists, and if any continuity can be assumed between my picture of those years and the America of to-day. I would ask whether there is still that sturdy confidence in the power to overcome all obstacles, and a boundless faith in the constitutional system of the great Republic, which I found in Roosevelt, in Taft, and in all America's leading men. Economically, and hence socially, the entire world is about to pass through great changes whose extent we cannot gauge.

The ideas on which reforming activity has been based in recent centuries have been discredited as a result of many disappointments. Faith in them has vanished, and no one understands clearly what can be put in their place. A substitute is to be seen in the hideous mask of Soviet Russia. There a system of social disorder obtains which annihilates the whole mental and spiritual life of the individual, every independent initiative, every endeavour towards great achievement; in a word, all individual character. Mankind sinks back under it into a colourless mass of mediocrity, destitute of all moral foundations, and lacking any higher ideal that might raise it above the level of a thinking machine.

A great question is before civilised humanity, to which a suitable answer must be found. Are America's prospects better or worse than those of old Europe?

Indisputably this great nation is passing through a crisis which perhaps goes deeper, and will be more difficult to overcome, than that of the Civil War, which threatened its stability in the 'sixties. May Providence bring forth leaders for it in this crisis similar to Abraham Lincoln, whom I mentioned above. May the native strength of the people carry them through this great trial in a spirit of vitality and confidence, such as has always been theirs till now. May the intellectual forces, which are so active in the blossoming of their literature, speak out concerning the signs of social disintegration everywhere obvious, in a way which will make the national character capable of resisting them. They must not be content with an artistic rendering of these signs of decay, and with the observance of complete detachment, but must throw their weight into the struggle against them.

A countryman of mine, who recently spent some time in New York, told me how every evening, at certain crowded points of the city, electric signs are shown with the inscription, *We shall see it through*. That is the real spirit of America.

CHAPTER VI

ROME YESTERDAY AND TO-DAY

WHOLE libraries have already been written about Rome by poets, historians, philosophers, statesmen, æstheticians, historians of art, in short by the representatives of every branch of knowledge. Yet the subject is never exhausted, because it continually renews itself. The Rome of to-day differs so much from that of yesterday, that there is still room, despite all these volumes, for things that have not been written, because it has not yet been possible to write them.

Yes, it is so indeed. To-day the visitor sees a new Rome, —or shall we say ancient Rome resurrected? With certain qualifications, this formula applies. In a changed form, much is now alive that one had looked upon as a mere memory, and much that appears new acquires an ancient spiritual significance, without losing any of its present-day power.

I saw Rome first in 1870. As a young man of twenty-four, I steeped myself in its manifold lessons, completed my æsthetic education and reached a stage of knowledge in the philosophy of history which sufficed me for many years. In the course of my later journeys, I have been able to watch the growth of the idea of Italian unity, as well as the conflict into which this has entered with the traditions and the never-ageing claims of Rome the Eternal, *Roma æterna*. I have experienced in my own mind a reaction to this conflict, for, even as a foreigner, I have been sensible of inward disagreement between the sympathy which I felt for Italy's national ideal and my unshakable attachment to the Rock of Peter. Rome, considered also from the æsthetic point of view, no longer presented a harmonious picture. It broke up into fragments, out of which I was not able to build up a whole, because it was evident that such a synthesis was impossible. It can easily be imagined what it meant to me when I saw the new Rome—or let us say ancient Rome awakened to life—released from these contradictions. I felt the harmony which seemed to have entered more completely than ever into all the elements of Rome's world significance.

This unity of all that constitutes her greatness is what is new in Rome. The new is built up of the old, but the old appears rejuvenated in the new. You can give yourself up entirely to the enjoyment of any of its parts, for these support one another instead of conflicting. There is an ancient Rome that is alive with youthful freshness, and a new city that is nourished on old experiences. One has here a synthesis of tradition and modernity, of the worship of the past with the consciousness of the future, such as is is to be met with nowhere else.

This new attitude, which is characteristic and specifically Roman, never struck me so forcibly as in November, 1932. I had been invited by the Accademia Reale d'Italia to take part in an international conference which it had summoned to discuss the European problem. To represent the political element, a number of statesmen were included in the deliberations besides men of learning, and so it happened that I and some colleagues from other countries found ourselves in a society of scholars,—like Saul among the prophets. I had, therefore, abundant opportunities to meet the leaders of Italian politics and learning, as well as to find out the impressions of other foreigners, and compare them with my own. I realised how fitting it was to discuss Europe in Rome, for Rome in fact made Europe.

The old Rome laid the foundations of political order in this continent, as they remain in outline to this day. She introduced all nations to the knowledge and understanding of Greek culture. A more recent Rome spread Christianity among men, and was the central point of an organisation which secured the purity and constancy of Christian faith. From here radiated the work undertaken by Christianity, whose effect was to put human values on a new basis, and to secure recognition for these in a reformed system of justice. This work is far from being completed, and the prosecution of it has, in fact, received its strongest encouragement from Papist Rome during our time, that is to say, since Leo XIII. From there, the great school of mediæval Christian philosophy was guided in its progress. As far as technical difficulties and the ever-recurring signs of a half-tamed barbarism permitted, Rome was a central point controlling the relations of people with people, and her influence and teaching prepared the way for the rise of international law. From Rome came the intellectual current which made the age of humanism and the Renaissance. These intellectual movements were associated with lamentable moral decadence, and for this reason led to a schism in the Church, which lessened the decisive influence hitherto exercised by Rome on the intellectual life of civilised man. There remained to her a spiritual control and binding ecclesiastical authority over such Christians as remained Catholics. As for the leadership in the intellectual life of the world, it was taken over alternately by the great Latin and Germanic nations, especially the French and the Germans; in mental achievement, Italy dropped for the time being behind. How much the Papacy still represented, though now reduced to a purely ecclesiastical power, was admitted by Napoleon I in a significant phrase. Immediately after the anti-Catholic outrages of the French Revolution, in the days when the Encyclopædists' philosophical doctrines were practically supreme, Napoleon gave the first Ambassador whom he sent to the Pope this brief order: "Deal with him as if he had an army of 500,000 men."

In fact, the moral strength of the Papacy, the solidarity of Church doctrine and internal discipline had all been restored, after the moral degeneracy of the Renaissance, by a far-reaching reform at the Council of Trent. An age of learning and faith set in for the Catholic Church, but, notwithstanding, her earlier position of supremacy in the intellectual life of mankind was not won back, and Italy's significance among the nations sank to its lowest ebb. Italian provinces became mere consolation prizes in the disputes of European dynasties. War and peace were made at the expense of Italian independence, and expropriated foreign dynasts were compensated with fragments of her soil. Under these degrading conditions, the idea of a unified Italy made slow progress, and not till the second half of the nineteenth century did it acquire the power to win through.

When I first arrived in Rome early in 1870, I found the atmosphere there one of conflict. The Papal State had already lost the greater part of its territory, but Rome, and a small area immediately around it, was still under the temporal rule of the Pope, thanks to the protection of France, who maintained a military occupation there. Her army was at once a symbol of French power, and the only real support for the shrunken temporal authority of the Holy Father, for the little papal army could not be compared with the military strength of the Italian Kingdom. It was obvious that this situation had not the slightest prospect of permanence. A change in French policy would be enough to end it, as actually happened after her defeat in 1871. In 1870, that is to say the year before, there was no sign of this change. The shrunken Papal State still existed, and a compromise seemed impossible between the desire of the Italians to occupy Rome as their capital and the unshakable conviction of leading Catholics that the Pope, as head of the world Church, could not dispense with the guarantee of independence offered by a temporal sovereignty. The principle upheld by the Papal Court was that a territorial sovereignty should be maintained as a holy duty of conscience and honour. Even after the accomplished fact of Rome's occupation by the Italian army and of her proclamation as capital of Italy, the Vatican maintained this principle for sixty more years and during three Pontificates, every compromise being rejected. The inner conflict produced by these mutually exclusive and warring currents was already noticeable at the beginning of 1870, when the last remnant of temporal power still remained to the Vatican. This authority had become so precarious that one already lived under the threat of its collapse.

In sharp contrast to this vacillating mood, the Catholic Church chose this moment for a tremendous display of her universal spiritual power. An event took place which had never happened since the Council of Trent, that is to say, for three hundred years. Pope Pius IX summoned an

Oecumenical Council in Rome, to make clear the position with regard to the Papacy's sphere of spiritual power. This was a remarkable demonstration to make at a moment when the Papacy was for practical purposes in a besieged city, and it proved how independent of all external power are the imperishable elements of the Church.

My first visit to Rome coincided with this situation. It can readily be imagined how all the problems which beset me during this visit affected my youthful mind. They touched upon my deepest convictions and stirred the most sacred cords of feeling. I found it hard to keep my mind sufficiently free to form even an average acquaintance with the historical and the æsthetic background of Rome. Under expert guidance I studied the old memorials of the pagan and Christian periods, as well as the collections and museums, the palaces and churches, in which the wonderful art treasures of the Eternal City are stored. I learnt much more, very much more, in a few weeks than elsewhere in years, but I never even attempted to arrange this new knowledge and experience into an organic whole. I did not attempt, either, to understand the connection between this great past and the events which were threatening, or actually happening before my eyes. This would have been difficult for maturer minds, and so it lasted for decades. Ancient Rome remained a splendid museum piece, modern Rome offered the spectacle of a violent conflict between the two powers residing in it, the Papacy and the Italian Crown. In the end, you understood the difficulties of a solution to the problem, and welcomed the modification brought about in the acuteness of the conflict by practical necessities. The idea of Rome was broken up into parts, having no spiritual bond, and it was impossible to obtain a harmonious general view. It was characteristic of the position that even a foreign visitor to the city, if he were a Catholic and a person of some consequence, had to choose whether he would present himself at the Vatican or the Quirinal, for one was not compatible with the other.

This picture is now entirely changed.

The great gulf between Papal and Italian Rome has been crossed. Both live peacefully together, and the spiritual conflict which darkened the life of many millions of Italians has disappeared. The Church has recognised Italy's claim to Rome as a capital, and the Italian State has respected the independence of Papal power, by recognising that the Pope has temporal authority within the territory of the Vatican. The most difficult problem with which the Church had to contend in defence of her external stability, and the Italian kingdom, in defence of its national life, has been solved. The warring souls have made peace.

Simultaneously, and arising out of the same spirit, a great change has taken place in the life of the Italian people. That likeable and gifted nation, inclined as it has been to indolence and the *dolce far niente*, and not over-fond of strict regulations, has become the most hard-working and best disciplined of all nations. The punctuality which one finds now in all official circles and public establishments might serve as a pattern. Nowhere does one meet with careless-ness, a casual attitude, or unpunctuality. Public safety leaves nothing to be desired, and you never hear Maffia or Camorra spoken of, where a few years ago it was necessary to take an armed guard if you went a few miles out of Palermo. Even the streets of the great cities speak of a discipline in the crowd whose like is to be found nowhere else. This has not by any means been achieved at the expense of happiness. On the contrary, cheerful faces are everywhere to be seen, and on all sides one meets with civility and confidence.

Hardly less significant is the change which has taken place in ancient Rome, the city of the Forum Romanum and the Capitol. This Rome has come out of its seclusion as a museum quarter and has taken on a new life. The modern city, and all Italy, in the proud awakening of their energies, have associated themselves with the national idea which these monuments recall. The thread of tradition leads back without a break to the spiritual legacy of the Roman Empire, which is no longer mere matter to be surveyed and dreamt about. For such things, the new Italy has no time. She is possessed by its active, living power, not, of course, with the object of reviving the desire for world domination, but in so far as this new Italy will not yield the palm to anyone. She wishes to be *prima inter pares* in the peaceful race for progress and advancement; in fact, she is anxious through her institutions to indicate a way of solving the problems of the world.

My dominating impression of Italy is what I would call the feeling of æsthetic satisfaction which is caused by this new harmony among the diverse elements included in the term "Rome." The creation of this psychological capital, the welding into a moral unity of the whole Italian nation, is perhaps the present Government's most imposing achievement. The introduction of ancient Roman thought into the most modern efforts to promote social welfare; the rousing of those great memories in the consciousness of the masses so successfully that, inspired by them, they accept with determination and joy the discipline and hard work which the system demands of all citizens; the reconciliation of intense Italian national feeling and revolutionary traditions connected with the campaign for Italian unity, with the immutable doctrines of the Catholic Church and a new eagerness of faith; even the master stroke by which the prestige of the Crown was brought as a unifying force into a reform movement that called itself revolutionary; in a word, the assembling of all psychological factors which influence the soul of the Italian people, in order that national energies should exert themselves to their very limit, is an achievement hardly to be equalled in history. For we must not forget that Fascism, though it bears the mark of an exceptional man, and though the terms "one-man rule," "dictatorship," "lack of freedom," are often applied to it, has the roots of its power in mass feeling, mass faith, and mass enthusiasm. Nothing proves better the greatness of Mussolini than that he has been able to found his personal authority on a broad popular basis. It is spoken of as a parallel system to that of Soviet Russia, because both wish to replace individualism in industry by organisation, that is to say, if we may use a common catchword, both practise a planned economy. It would hardly be possible to imagine a profounder cleavage than exists between these two kinds of planned economy. The Soviet domination is founded upon the overthrow of all existing moral factors; religion, family, national tradition, accepted authorities, all must be destroyed, and communal life be built exclusively on a basis of Marxian materialism.

In a contrary spirit, Fascist Italy is striving, as we have seen, not only to maintain, but to strengthen, the traditional moral principles from which she draws the impulse to develop her fullest powers. The planned economy of Soviet Russia looks upon individual men as mechanical parts in the collective process of production, excluding individual initiative, responsibility, and ambition. In that system, the individual loses all significance, and practically all chance of distinguishing himself. Under it, mankind would necessarily relapse into a colourless monotony of despair, for every psychological impulse to advance and to achieve greater things would be lacking. It is difficult to imagine the spiritual retrogression which would ensue, and the moral nihilism, if that system were to continue long. Fascism, on the other hand, organises work with the object of preventing any relapse, even of individuals, below the level which is proper to man. It keeps open the path by which anyone may attain, through moral strength and conspicuous achievement, to positions of distinction. Without weakening individual character, from which all great deeds spring, it seeks to fight the abuses of individualism. The Fascist organisation, as is natural, is still in many respects in the experimental stage. It has certainly not said its last word, but its first has been said decisively, and in such a way that even those must listen who do not feel themselves drawn to the system. The results already attained, and especially their effect on the spirit of the people which anyone may observe, show clearly the irreconcilable contradiction which divides Fascism from Communism. The remark of a clever woman who spent some time in Soviet Russia, and then expressed what she had observed in a sentence, struck me forcibly: "I never saw a smiling face there."

Compare Italy, where on all sides we meet gaiety and a self-confident love of life. It is true that we see even there the ill effects of the world economic crisis, especially in the northern provinces, whose economic situation resembles most our own. There is nothing, however, to be seen of the collapse and misery whose proofs meet us here in Hungary at every step. Life in the streets of Rome does not come short in any respect of what it used to be. In those parts of the city where I walked, I saw no such thing as a tenantless shop, nor any announcement of a sale as the result of a business closing down. One may also observe that in the darkest aspect of our world crisis, namely unemployment, Italy is the most fortunately placed of all nations. I have before me a volume published last October by the Ministry of Labour, being one of its periodical reports, and I read that the total number of unemployed in Italy in September, 1932, was 949,499—710,000 men and 240,000 women—compared with 945,927 in August. The increase was therefore only 3,600, although from August to September it is usual to record an increase of from 40,000 to 50,000, owing to the cessation of many agricultural tasks. The figures for 1932 prove, therefore, that other branches of the national economy were able to absorb the labour released from the land. Moreover, the total figure for unemployment, compared with the population, gives a smaller percentage than is to be found in any other country.

I do not feel competent to give an opinion as to the state of Italy's national finances, but I may perhaps draw attention to the fact that the Italian lira lost none of its value at a time when there occurred that apparently impossible thing, the fall of the English pound. I repeat, however, that these remarks lay no claim to being economic judgments, but represent only my personal views.

I cannot pass on without mentioning the impression which I received of the tremendous personality, whose far-reaching power of suggestion, genius, and strength of will form a background to those aspects of Italian life which I have here sketched. I speak of the Duce. This word as a term for Mussolini has passed into everyday speech, not through any decree of etiquette, but by spontaneous habit, as representing a truth. Everyone sees in him the "Duce," the leader, and has unlimited confidence in the manner in which he fulfils his calling. This title gives a companionable feeling to those in subordinate positions, and decreases the distance between powerful and weak. That is thoroughly Italian. Even in the army, discipline takes on a less rigid character than in northern lands. The Italian cannot do without warmth, either in the material world or in the spiritual.

Mussolini would not be the greatest, and most Italian, of living Italians if he did not appreciate this quality of his people, nor feel the necessity of exercising his power with a kind of inward ardour, just as the people feel the necessity, for their part, of introducing this psychic element into their manner of obedience. This mingling of a kindlier spirit has had an incalculable effect in softening the harshness of an exceedingly strict leadership, without introducing any trace of weakness.

238

What were my personal impressions of the Duce? Have they been sufficiently various to enable me to form a picture of his human aspect that could elucidate the character of this great leader, and make it easier to understand him?

I would answer this question in the affirmative.

I was not in the happy position of Emil Ludwig, who spent many hours in conversation with him and recorded his answers to a carefully prepared questionnaire. However, I do not think that this is the right way to understand a great personality, because the questioner is free to choose his own questions, and the portrait he draws in this way will contain as much of himself as his subject, if not more. The things which come to the fore are those that seem important to the questioner, and much that is most typical of the other's character remains unstressed, and perhaps quite unmentioned. Altogether, I have three times had the privilege of talking to Mussolini alone, and our conversations have amounted to perhaps the same number of hours. During this relatively short time, he did not sit to me, if I may use the expression, as though I was painting his portrait. He had not to answer questions put to him with this object, for each time the conversation turned upon matters of vital concern to our peoples, which were therefore closely associated with his life's work. He knew that I did not trouble him out of mere curiosity, but that it was most important for me, and indirectly for my country, to have exact knowledge of his views on the great questions concerning which I often officially undertook international missions. He spoke openly, and with the complete trust which is required by the common interests and extremely friendly relations of our countries. The picture which I formed of him in this way cannot possibly be complete, but at least it is true to nature.

First of all, I would like to recall a few details, unimportant perhaps in themselves, yet highly characteristic. At my first visit, I opened the conversation by directly asking how much time he could give me. He at once answered: "To-day only half an hour, but if that is not enough, come and see me——" he scrutinised a heavy notebook, then made an entry—"the day after to-morrow at this time;" and so it happened. When I appeared two days later, we took up the thread of conversation without any preamble, at the exact point where we had dropped it. That this should happen in any case was quite natural, because my talks with Mussolini were the most important part of my visit to Rome, but that he should remember the details of a conversation with me when his brain had been occupied meanwhile with countless difficult transactions and problems, and that he could continue it as though there had been no interruption, is a most exceptional feat. It allows me to count these two visits as one. As a parallel, I would like to mention how my last visit to him in November, 1932, was announced. Early in November, our

Legation received word that Mussolini would see me. My visit to Rome was planned to last from the 14th to the 20th of the month. On November 4th, I heard from the Legation that the Duce would expect me at half-past five on the 15th. I presented myself on that day without further notification, and was at once admitted to him, but I had the impression that he was expecting me. It is this exact time-table and the gift of concentrating on the subject in hand, to the momentary exclusion of all others, which make it possible for him to accomplish the gigantic tasks which fall to the Duce's lot.

As regards Mussolini's conversation, one is surprised by the informal simplicity, the directness, the clarity and decision which free his remarks from all trace of pose. The great ambitions which he cherishes for his people, and the confidence which he places in their many-sided ability, do not prejudice in any way his practical judgment of the political factors with which he has to reckon. I have seldom met a man in whom justifiable self-confidence is so completely balanced by freedom from illusions. This is a most important point. The secret of the statesman of genius whose acts are not only dazzling but lasting, consists in a clear recognition of the attainable and its limits. If we say of a great man that he can achieve anything he desires, we really mean that he is clever enough never to desire anything that he cannot achieve. The great danger to a power that has no counterpoise, and is not exposed to free criticism, lies in the fact that its possessor loses his clear vision of the limits of the possible. There are numerous examples of this, sometimes of a very tragic kind, among the great figures of history. It is enough to mention Napoleon. Human nature is imperfect even in the greatest men, and cannot endure an excess of power without giddiness. There is no trace of this in Mussolini. It is to be supposed that he meets with the desirable measure of criticism amongst the able men who surround him; but, in any case, he is protected from the perils of power which I have described by the exceptional balance of his abilities, and by the predominance in him of communal, rather than subjective, feeling. However paradoxical it may sound, one can say of him that his subjectivity is of an objective kind. He regards himself entirely as the instrument of a great purpose, and his whole mental and bodily regimen is directed to assuring the greatest possible efficiency for this instrument.

This monumental aspect of his character communicates itself to his speech. Every sentence is a thought, and every thought part of a great aim. One covers more in half an hour's talk with him than in conversing with other people for hours. You have an irresistible impression, which even the most sceptical person must share, that this man is absolutely sincere and genuine; and more than this, that he is good, actually kind, able to sympathise with his fellow-men, and no harsher towards them than his great work demands; but then, indeed, pitiless. This direct personal impression was confirmed by all those who know him well or work in continual contact with him. My emphasis on the kindly, human aspect of his character is not mere sentimentality, for that aspect also is a source of power to him. He is one of those great men for whom we feel not only admiration, but genuine liking as well, and this is an element in the incomparable power which he has over men.

The idea that one forms of him is therefore one of complete harmony, of a rare balance of abilities. Over and above this, he possesses another great source of strength, namely his origin and career. The son of humble people, as a boy and as a young man he lived in the world of the poorer classes. He has known privations, or at least been able to observe them at close quarters. He shared the bitterness of poor intellectuals fighting for their material existence. He knew, to put it in a word, the actual life, and the whole life, of the vast majority of mankind. What do we know of such things, who have been born among the so-called upper ten thousand, and have lived their life? Theoretically, we know that there are poorer classes, fellow-men who are exposed to privations and the hardships of life. We have a certain sympathy for them, and busy ourselves in their interest with plans for reform, but only knowledge gained by personal experience eats into the bones and the marrow. He alone is entitled vigorously to preach patience and a refusal of the idea of revolution who can say to the masses: "I know your distress, for it has been mine, but I know also the way to a better future, which is not that of violent revolution, but of organised co-operation."

There is no doubt that the great man in whom all these elements which went to a successful struggle with fate are united, is responsible for a very large share of the triumphs which Fascism boasts in Italian life. Out of this statement arises the question as to whether the system can survive its founder, whether its institutions will have the power to continue functioning when Mussolini is no more.

This is a problem facing Italy which weighs on no one more oppressively than on the Duce.

It is difficult for a foreigner to give anything like a valid answer. Once more, I can only instance certain impressions which allow of a more favourable forecast than one can usually make concerning institutions that depend on an outstanding personal character. This is possible because, in Mussolini's case, the outstanding man has passed, to a much greater extent than usual, into the national character, and has become a kind of institution. Mussolini has used his great power of suggestion, not only to make the masses follow him, but also to instil into them ideas and feelings which have a universal bearing. The cult of ancient Rome, the realisation of Italy's world mission, the beneficial effect of strict order and discipline, and of an economic system based on co-operation, the restored harmony of faith and patriotism—these are all motives of a lasting kind, which have entered deeply into the national consciousness, and can continue without a personal cult. It must also be remarked that the so-called Fascist Revolution was organised by the usually indolent majority, who want order and calm, against the always active minority consisting of the friends of subversion. To build up such a system was Mussolini's first great deed. It has enabled the orderly elements to remain in control at a critical moment, and through it Italy was snatched back from the abyss of anarchy into which she threatened to fall. The need for maintaining such an organisation, and the memory of the frightful danger which was avoided thanks to it, must have sunk into the minds of the people. Fascism has not yet said its last word on the subject of organisation, and it is certain that the progress still to be made in a creative direction will achieve stronger objective guarantees for its survival.

On the one hand, this survival will depend on its economic institutions continuing to work successfully, and on the other, it will depend upon the course of world economic and social movements. No one can deny that the capitalist system is passing through a severe crisis, from which it can only be saved by a radical transformation, with the object of alleviating social inequalities. Anyone who is trying to find the means of bringing about this progress cannot remain indifferent to all that the present régime has done in Italy. When Mussolini made the bold statement in his last speech at Milan that all Europe would be Fascist in a few years, this was not to be taken literally, but only in the sense that the *carta di lavoro* and the corporative institutions of present-day Italy are indications of the social progress that will be generally necessary. It is therefore possible that some kind of agreement will be reached in world movements which would be decidedly favourable to the continuance of the Fascist system.

Perhaps I have already over-stepped the limit of mere impressions in these remarks. Nevertheless, I am convinced that the illustrious participants in the conference on Europe organised by the Accademia Reale d'Italia were occupied with similar observations and thoughts. Not for nothing had this assembly come together in a Roman atmosphere. The Italian speakers declared that institutions were maturing in their country which deserved the notice of leading men in all European lands, and these statements obviously impressed the foreigners, because they were given opportunities to observe the results. It was extraordinary how the influence of the learned atmosphere which reigned undisturbed in this gathering affected the treatment of the most ticklish problems of European politics. I myself touched upon one of these. I put forward the indefensible circumstances created by the peace treaties as the reason—and I developed this theme— why mutual confidence, no less than the moral unity, and even the economic recovery, of Europe seemed impossible. The answer given me by Michael Politis, a famous Greek lawyer and politician, on behalf of what I would call the other party, was conceived in just such an objective spirit, and it opened the way to an understanding, in a manner which would be unthinkable to-day at a political gathering. This leads naturally to the idea that repeated scientific discussions of European problems, where questions would be considered in a dispassionate light, without preconceived theories and political partisanship, would be very well adapted to create a general agreement among the best brains, whose influence would in time prove irresistible. We all underwent a kind of change in this assembly, whose meetings were not held in public, thereby preventing any desire to appeal to the gallery. We breathed an air exalted and Roman. It made no difference that we were so busy all day as hardly to see anything of Rome itself. Never have I felt the influence of the eternal city so powerfully as in those days. Of course we were in constant touch with outstanding Romans, among whom I will only mention the President of the Academy, Marconi, who has overcome the obstacle to contact between human beings over long distances, and who is now engaged on new discoveries, which should make oral communications still simpler and easier throughout the world. He is also an important political figure. Belonging to Mussolini's most intimate circle of friends, and equally well received at the Vatican, he personifies an upward striving which fills the spirit of Italy to-day.

This does not exhaust the sum of important impressions I gathered in Rome during November, 1932. I wished to avail myself of this opportunity to pay my respects to the head of my Church, and was received in private audience by Pope Pius XI. This was the third Pius whom I had visited in the Vatican. I have already remarked upon the great difference in the situations obtaining when I was granted my first audience in 1870 and my last, a year ago. The realisation of this contrast almost choked me, as I passed along the same corridors and halls, between the same uniforms and cassocks, among all the familiar outward show, and found myself before Pius XI in the same study where, sixty-two years earlier, Pius IX had given me his blessing. In the essence of things nothing indeed was changed, and after countless years that which the Catholic seeks and finds in the head of his Church will remain still unaltered. The Pope's power in his Church continues to be the same, the teaching whose chief guardian he is remains the same, but how much that is new can be introduced into these unchanging things! In his time, I had found Pius IX struggling with a great problem, that of the temporal power of the Pope, whose defence and vindication against material supremacy he looked upon as a holy task and as an affair of honour, since it concerned, not a personal possession, but a source of power to the

Church. In his own eyes, he was a mere beneficiary in control, whose duty was to hand on his power undiminished to his successor. After the experiences of sixty years had proved the impossibility of restoring the old system, Pius XI welcomed the new order with decision, and turned to the future rather than to a past which could not be brought back.

To break in this way the tradition of three great Popes required an unusual strength of decision and willingness to accept great responsibilities. In all respects, Pius XI is a man of far-reaching decisions. He is commonly described as an autocrat, and it is certain that everything he does comes from his own initiative. It needed a strong man to carry out the great work of reconciliation with Italy, no less than to act as a representative of the Church as against Mussolini, and keep him alive to the necessity of reaching an agreement. It was an act of Providence to bring these two personalities together in Rome's history.

In other ways, the present head of the Church has given proof of his active energy. He is helped by the fact that the unity of all minds within the Church has never been so complete as in our day. She is, indeed, harassed by persecution, and in many countries has to contend with external enemies—to cite only Mexico; but internally there is no trace of conflicting intellectual movements, such as Pius IX still had to fight. The technical progress of science is also of great service to the central Church authority. The Church has every reason to bless science, which makes it possible for the Pope in a broadcast speech to address hundreds of missions at once, and to be always informed of events in the most distant part of the earth. How much more effectively can the supreme ecclesiastical authorities act nowadays, when things that were spoken, or took place, at Peking in the morning are known in the afternoon, compared with the time when months passed before the news of important events could be received from much less distant areas! I will only mention two of Pius XI's remaining achievements. In the extra-European mission fields, such as China, Central Asia, and India, he has created a hierarchy of native priests, and has already ordained a considerable number of Chinese and Indian Bishops. He adopted this course in the wise belief that the success of missions is greatly furthered if those who bring the new teaching bear the stamp of their own people in everything not contrary to Christianity, if they love and honour their native traditions, and if also, by the fact of belonging to the people, they exclude all suspicion that they are at the same time representing foreign political interests. Nevertheless, it required an unusual strength of decision to place such confidence in the neophytes of Christianity. The other great lead given by the present Pope, which I would like to mention, is his keen support of social reform. In this respect, he is treading in the foot-steps of his great predecessor, Leo XIII, whose Encyclical

"Rerum novarum" was a landmark in the social evolution of the last century. Pius, however, widens his scope with the help of the newest scientific discoveries, and thus carries the Church to the head of this movement as a driving force and a determining factor in it, at a moment when the capitalist system is passing through its most critical stage. It was an experience to have the privilege of exchanging ideas with this Pope, and I left his study deeply moved, but inwardly strengthened. Like the national Italian Rome, Rome of the Vatican is the centre of great decisions—even great in a human sense—and inspired by profundity of thought. A complete vision of *Roma æterna* was now before my eyes.

Late in the afternoon of the day on which I left Rome, I sought out once more the point whence I have my favourite view of the city, namely, the Park of Monte Pincio. A setting sun was flooding the scene with his red light: on one side rose the commanding dome of St. Peter's, and on the other, the Colosseum and the Capitol. All Rome was symbolised there. I let my eyes rest on this picture, and, without defining my thoughts, I took it in like some sublime work of music, and retained it in my mind. As darkness fell, a light continued to shine in me such as the idea of Rome throws across our dark times.

CHAPTER VII

HOW PEACE WAS MADE AFTER THE GREAT WAR

I DO not intend to criticise the contents of the peace treaties, but to describe the events which took place when they were drawn up. In so far as the treaty with Hungary is concerned, I took a personal, though, of course, a passive, part in its making. All the same, I was present, and the experience remains a fragment of history. It should be of some value to describe this event from what I would call the anecdotal point of view.

By the late autumn of 1919, after my country had overthrown Bolshevism and had been swamped by a Rumanian invasion, a government was set up whose authority was recognised throughout the country, though it lacked any legal basis, and with which the Allied Powers were prepared to negotiate officially for the signing of peace. This government consisted of representatives of all parties, under the leadership of Károly Huszár, who belonged to the Christian People's party. It had two principal objects, one of which was concerned with internal and the other with external affairs. The first was to summon, by means of a universal franchise, a national assembly to decide upon the internal management of the country, which was in a state of complete disorder. The other task was to send a peace delegation to Paris, whose duty there would be to receive the decisions of the victors, represented by the Supreme Allied Council, and to draw them up in treaty form. I was chosen to be the leader of this peace delegation, and, as public opinion in my country supported the choice made by the provisional government, I could not refuse this saddest of duties, though I had no illusions as to there being any possibility of my securing some mitigation of our lot. This fate had been realised already through the occupation by our ex-enemies of great areas of Hungarian soil. The spirit which I was up against declared itself at the first step I had to take on that thorny path.

I was then living with my family at our former estate of Eberhard, near Pozsony, which has been taken from me by the Treaty of Trianon. I had come to Budapest for a short time only, to assist in the negotiations which led to setting up the Huszár Cabinet. The part of Hungary in which my estate was situated had already been occupied by the Czechs, and was actually under Czech control. Through the local Czech authorities, I received in the middle of December an urgent request from the Hungarian government to come to Budapest. The Czech authorities had no objection to my travelling. In Budapest I learnt for the first time that it was suggested I should take over the mission to Paris. After I had accepted, some days were spent in negotiations concerning the personnel of the peace delegation, and in fixing the date of its departure. January 5th, 1920, was selected, by arrangement with the delegates. When all this had been settled, I naturally wanted to return to Eberhard, and spend Christmas there with my family. To my great surprise, I met with an abrupt refusal from the Czech government, whose motive was expressed as follows in the original French: "Il est inadmissible qu'un personnage désigné pour soutenir les intérêts de la Hongrie contre ceux de l'Etat tchécoslovaque puisse séjourner sur le territoire de ce dernier." In vain I appealed to the representatives of the Entente against this decree, which was absurd from the point of view of international law. They probably sympathised with me, but they did not help me. The decree stood, and I was not allowed to go home. As soon as this was decided, my family applied to the Pozsony authorities for permission to spend Christmas with me in Budapest. This also was bluntly refused—as we were told, on direct instructions from Prague. I withhold comment. If anyone can find a satisfactory explanation for such wilful interference with family life during the favourite Christian festival, it is not for me to disabuse him; for my part I have found none. I had, therefore, to remain in Budapest, the only consolation for my loneliness being the presence of my son, who could not leave Budapest, because he was a liaison officer at the English Military Mission.

January 5th arrived. The Hungarian peace delegation was fairly numerous, for we foresaw that a written answer would have to be prepared to the so-called offer of peace, and this would require, in addition to the chief delegates, a number of experts and adequate technical advisers. Among the chief delegates, I will mention Sándor Popovic, afterwards President of the National Bank of Hungary, and formerly President of the Austro-Hungarian Bank, Count István Bethlen, Pál Teleki, Imre Csáky, Tibor Kállay and Lajos Walkó, who have all subsequently taken a leading part in Hungarian politics, but most of whom were already well-known politicians. Excellent legal and military help was allotted to us. Both the Hungarian government and I myself had been at the greatest pains to secure for us as representatives the best intellects in the country, with regard to political, financial, economic, legal and general technical matters. However slight was the prospect of successful negotiations, in fact of negotiations at all, the honour of the country had to be preserved under all circumstances. Our delegation travelled to Paris in a special train, whose formation was no small task for the plundered Hungarian railways, since the work of reconstruction had not even begun. They succeeded, however, and our train looked as if normal conditions had obtained. All the passengers were comfortably provided for, and they even found a Pullman car which served for discussions on the journey.

These discussions were interrupted at every large station along the Hungarian line in a way that was very touching, but at the same time, painful. Everywhere there were large or small deputations, and sometimes crowds of poor people, who filled the waiting rooms at the stations, and whose spokesmen wished us God-speed, declaring the confidence of the Hungarian people that we would undoubtedly succeed in winning acceptable terms of peace for our country. It cut us to the quick to see this trust and confidence, and to realise the enthusiasm with which their words were uttered. We knew only too well that there was not the slightest reason for such hopes, that we were faced already with an accomplished fact and that we went on our forlorn mission out of no more than a painful sense of duty. Occasionally, doubts assailed us as to whether it would be better, after all, to do as had been seriously suggested to me, namely, sign the conditions presented to us in Paris without negotiating, and in this way make still more obvious the coercion that was being put upon us. After careful consideration, we decided that we would not follow this advice, because one can never be absolutely sure in such matters, and even a minute hope carried with it the duty at least of attempting to obtain something. What a painful contrast there was between our mood of hopeless duty and the enthusiastic confidence which cheered us on! In replying to the speeches addressed to me, I could only speak the truth, saying that I neither promised nor expected a success, and could do no more than give my assurance, once and for all, that the honour of our country would not suffer.

On the journey, we were accompanied by one or two officers of the English and Italian Military Mission in Budapest. We were on the friendliest terms with these officers, who had lived in Budapest for some time, as we were with all the members of the Military Mission, who had come to Budapest full of prejudices and antipathy, only to undergo a complete change of opinion after spending a little while in our country. This was especially so with the Italian General Graziani, who had assumed a very abrupt demeanour at the beginning of his official duties, but, after a few weeks of personal experience, formed such an attachment to our country that everyone was sorry to see him go when his mission was over. The etiquette observed by the French was very different from that of the military delegates of other countries. Their principle was that they would be dealing with an enemy until the peace treaty had been signed, and hence all friendliness beyond the demands of common courtesy was undesirable. No sooner had we reached Paris than we realised that this rule was to be maintained.

A French officer had been sent to meet us at the frontier, and from him we received the order—I forget in what form, but certainly as politely expressed as possible—that we could not yet shake hands, but must limit our greeting to the curt bow usual between utter strangers. And that was what actually happened. Our arrival in Paris took place after a railway journey of forty-eight hours, in the early morning of January 7, and was so arranged that our special train came into a deserted station. A small Military Commission—we called them our warders—was there to meet us, at whose head was Colonel Henry, who afterwards turned out to be a most kindly and benevolent man, though he received us as we got out of the carriage with merely ceremonial military salute, which we returned in a like manner. As the leader of the delegation, I entered an official car with him, and the officers were divided accordingly among the remaining members of the delegation. Quarters had been prepared for us at Neuilly, a suburb of Paris lying in the middle of the Bois de Boulogne, where we were to stay at the Hôtel "Château de Madrid," which is accustomed in the summer-time to shelter much less serious guests. During the drive from the station, I told Colonel Henry, somewhat naïvely, that I would like to visit certain people in Paris who were old French friends of mine, and he answered that he regretted this would be impossible. We had, so he told me, complete freedom of movement in Neuilly and the Bois de Boulogne, but were asked never to visit Paris itself without informing him. If a member of the delegation expressed this wish he would see that a car was placed at our disposal, and that we were provided with an adequate escort, *"afin qu'on ne manque pas de respect!*" We would not be allowed to pay visits in Paris, or to meet anyone, without his authority. In other words, we were interned in Neuilly. We could only enter Paris under the eye of a detective and with special permission, and we were allowed no visitors. All this was strictly carried out, though with the maintenance of formal politeness. Once a young journalist who belonged to our delegation, trusting to his obscurity, attempted to travel unnoticed to Paris by tram; at the last stopping-place before the Barrière de l'Etoile, he was peremptorily ordered by an unknown man to leave the tramcar. This man announced himself as a police agent, and, without more ado, ordered the culprit back to Neuilly. I received from the military authorities who were in charge of the foreign peace delegations an order to send the young man home at once, for the incident would otherwise lead to regrettable explanations. I would emphasise the fact that we had no complaint to make of any violation of the rules of courtesy by the French officers entrusted with our supervision. On the contrary, when we had been there some time, our relations became less tense, but the rules of the internment system to which we were subjected remained the same. We grew accustomed to them, thanks to the very cordial feeling between the members of our delegation. The same intense grief for the fate of our country, and for our inability to help her, dominated us all in a similar way.

Anything that might otherwise have divided us yielded to this supreme sensation. The area within which we were free was sufficiently large, and at that season sufficiently deserted, to allow us a variety of walks, during which no one so much as looked askance at us; although after a fortnight in the streets and coffee-houses and little restaurants in and about Neuilly, which we visited from time to time, every child knew us. I would almost say that we were accorded exceptional treatment in that locality. It happened only once that three members of the delegation, who were taking a walk in the Bois de Boulogne and had reached a deserted part of the forest, were insulted by the cry "Les sales Boches!" shouted at them from behind by a pedestrian. This pedestrian was no other than myself. I had caught sight of my friends, though they had not seen me, and I wanted to amuse myself by watching how they would react to this friendly greeting. They behaved in the proper way, namely by ignoring it, but that evening at dinner, to my great amusement, they related what had happened to them, saying that we could not be sure of our peace after all. Amusement became general when I revealed myself as the cause of this solitary insult suffered by our delegation during their long stay at Neuilly.

Our visit began with the performance of certain formalities, among others the mutual presentation of credentials, and this led at once to a characteristic incident. When our opponents' credentials were handed to us, I noticed that those of the American representative were missing. I naturally addressed a letter to the President of the Supreme Council, who was no other than Clemenceau, drawing attention to this omission. In answer to this I received—which was less natural—an almost rude reply: "If we wanted to make trouble," ran Clemenceau's answer, "we had better say that we would not negotiate at all," and in that case they would know how to deal with us. This letter aroused consternation in our circle because of its unusual tone, and I tried to dissipate the bad feeling with an anecdote. I told a story about a Tyrolese peasant whom an artist wished to paint, while on a visit among his mountains, because he had a "head full of character." The peasant related this to his old wife, and added, "I'm blowed if I know what an 'ead of character is, but whatever it means, I took good care to box 'is ears for 'im." This was apparently Clemenceau's method as well, whenever he did not understand anything. My answer to his charming "whatever it means" communication was very definite. I could not imagine how Monsieur le Président had ever formed the idea that we wished to delay the fulfilment of our task. If we had not had a sincere desire to negotiate, we would never have come to Paris. Since we had also to make peace with America, it was natural that we should wish to ensure the presence of an American representative. The incident was in any case at an end, for the American credentials had been handed to us meanwhile. I was anxious to make Clemenceau understand that his letter had met with no success, if he thought to intimidate us by it. In a situation such as ours, to hold one's head proudly is a rule from which there must be no flinching. Later on in this introductory correspondence, I wrote to Clemenceau asking if we might be granted the opportunity of personal negotiation, instead of receiving a written statement of the peace conditions, such as was sent to defeated States whose delegations had been in contact with the Supreme Council before our own. In answer to this letter, the only reply I received was an invitation to present ourselves at the Quai d'Orsay one morning in the course of the next few days, to receive the terms of peace. It was explained to me that I might be accompanied, as far as I remember, by ten members of the Hungarian delegation. We, of course, presented ourselves punctually at the hour mentioned, and were shown into a large waiting room, from which a door led directly into the room where the Supreme Council was already sitting, and where the remaining events were to take place.

This was a lengthy room, down one long side of which, with their backs turned to the five or six windows that lighted it, the members of the Supreme Council were sitting on a platform, in the following order: England, represented by Lloyd George, Lord Curzon and Bonar Law; Italy, represented by Nitti; then Japan. America had already withdrawn from the general peace negotiations, and had also refused to deal directly with us. At the head of the room, Clemenceau was sitting in front of a table, surrounded by several members of the French Cabinet and a crowd of senior officials of the French Ministries concerned. Here also were crowded the by no means large number of official reporters and stenographers. At a little distance from Clemenceau's Presidential seat, arm-chairs were set out for me and other members of the Hungarian delegation taking part in the ceremony, while in front of mine stood a table. This arrangement had the very considerable disadvantage for me that I could not see the faces of the Allied representatives, apart from Clemenceau's, for all of them had their backs turned to the light, and only their outlines were recognisable. We bowed to one another without speaking, and when we had all taken our places, Clemenceau spoke a few words to me, which amounted to no more than an announcement of the handing over to Hungary of the suggested peace terms. ("Le traité de paix proposé à la Hongrie.") The terms were handed over at once by a senior official. It was not without inward bitterness that I noticed the euphemism employed by Clemenceau when he spoke of an offer of peace "proposed to Hungary," for we knew only too well that he was dictating his terms. Of course, I could only receive the "offer" with a silent bow, for Clemenceau at once proceeded to make us the following announcement, which I must quote from memory, but which I can trust myself to repeat almost word for word: "Monsieur le Président"—this was how he always addressed me—"you have asked the Supreme Council for permission to make a speech about the situation of Hungary. The Supreme Council has unanimously decided to grant your request. There can, of course, be no question of a discussion. I shall, therefore, ask you, Monsieur le Président, to mention the day on which it would be convenient to you to make this statement."

I replied as follows: "I thank you, Monsieur le Président, for your information and the Supreme Council for their compliance, but I must observe that there has been a misunderstanding, for what I desired was not so much to make a speech as to take part in a discussion. Since the wishes of the Supreme Council in this matter appear to be final, I gratefully accept your offer. As regards the time of the meeting at which you will be so kind as to listen to me, I have no other request to make than that we should be allowed at least two days, in order to acquaint ourselves thoroughly with the contents of the terms of peace. After this interval, I shall be at the service of the Supreme Council on any day they may choose to suit their own convenience."

To this Monsieur Clemenceau, observing that the other members of the Council were nodding their heads in agreement, informed us that we would be expected at the same time in the morning three days hence.

Count Apponyi speaking at a Conference in Paris

Our first meeting with the Supreme Council was at an end. It had not really disappointed me, for I had never seriously hoped that we would be granted a real oral discussion, and, in fact, I had only requested it *"pour l'acquit de ma conscience."* What I had actually obtained was of no great practical value, but I could not refuse it, and, rather than worry over the inadequacy of a speech without a discussion, it was my duty to prepare this statement of our case with the greatest care. It was no less important to insure that on the day, and at the hour, appointed for my speech, I should be in the best possible frame of mind, and have my nerves under control. This last is easier said than done, but I felt I could depend upon what I had learnt by experience, that I never speak in public without emotion—even to-day, after sixty years' practice— although after the first few minutes of my speech, my nervous system would become completely calm, and a feeling of absolute confidence would come over me. I prayed to God that it would be so this time, for the audience before whom I had to speak, my relations with them, and my position before the assembly whom I had to impress, were all so completely new to me and attended with such difficulties, that no certain conclusion could be drawn from past experience. I devoted extreme care to the preparation of my statements, for in them I had to explain how utterly grotesque were the terms of peace which had been drawn up for us. I tried to express the great amount which I had to say as concisely and clearly as possible, but I did not compose an outline either in French or English, in both of which languages I expected to be called upon to speak. I could not achieve the necessary calm of mind to write or to dictate. Only the skeleton of my speech was prepared. As for the text, it would have to develop as I went along from the inspiration of the moment, and from any magnetic contact with the audience which I might succeed in establishing. I decided upon the tone which should dominate my speech. There was to be no sentimentality, no lamentations, no appeal to the charity of the victorious Powers, and especially no emotionalism of any kind, but a dry and, as far as possible, a lucid statement of facts, whose natural pathos would work its effect.

As I stepped into the room at the appointed hour, I felt again very strongly the unique character of the situation. I was to address an audience among whom there was not the slightest sympathetic element, an audience of enemies in the technical sense of the word, and for the most part of men ill-disposed towards us, with a slight admixture of indifferent listeners. I was saved from a feeling of complete isolation only by the fragment of our Hungarian delegation which was allowed to accompany me. In them, at any rate, I had ten or twelve companions who were possessed by entirely the same feelings as were uppermost in my mind. To me, they were a symbol of the Hungarian nation for whom I was about to speak.

This thought steeled my nerves for the trial which they would have to undergo.

I have already mentioned that the arrangement of the room made it impossible for me to see the faces of that particular section of the audience from whom I expected less hostile prejudice, namely the English, the Italians, and the Japanese. I stood face to face only with Clemenceau and his staff, and this part of the audience could not or would not hide their far from friendly attitude when I began my speech. In front of me were some malevolently serious faces, and others that wore a mocking smile. I could not be in any doubt as to the kind of prejudice with which my words would be received.

When Clemenceau invited me to begin my speech, I rose to do as he requested, whereupon he asked me very courteously to remain seated. I declined his offer by appealing to my Parliamentary habits. As a matter of fact, I prefer to stand, rather than sit, when addressing any considerable audience.

I began without any introduction by stating that the terms of peace proposed to us were completely unacceptable, and that I would demonstrate this with regard to their principal demands. I at once noticed that this dry tone, avoiding all sentimentality, came as a surprise to my listeners, or at least those of them whose impressions I could observe, and that it reacted not unfavourably on their mood. Very soon, I felt that I was amply com-

pensated for my inability to watch the expressions of most
of my audience by being enabled to read in Clemenceau's
face even the slightest reactions which my speech provoked. On the whole, I was able to perceive a change
taking place in his attitude. He was apparently not
displeased with me as a speaker, and consequently his face
soon lost the expression of mockery which at first he had
not been able to suppress, despite an affectation of politeness. His features took on, little by little, almost a benevolent look. At all events, his eyes left me as seldom as
mine left him. I had been speaking for about ten minutes
when Clemenceau interrupted me with the remark that
my speech would now be translated into English. The
interruption had been made at an opportune moment, but
it affected me unpleasantly by disturbing the organic
structure of my observations. I said that if Monsieur le
Président had no objection, I would myself undertake the
English translation, for I preferred to carry on in French to
the end, and then, after a pause, to deliver my speech as a
whole in English. Clemenceau did not accept this. It
would be rather too long, he said, for the gentlemen who
did not understand French to listen to the whole speech
without knowing what it contained. What could I do
except bow to the President's decision and obey his
wishes? It was left to me to decide at what points I should
break off, and in the course of my address I had to change
over four or five times from the rhythm of the French

language to that of the English, and from English back to French, which proved a very troublesome addition to the mental strain I already had to endure. Fortunately, I was able to overcome this obstacle without allowing the carefully prepared unity in the construction of my observations to suffer, or any failing of power to be apparent in my speech. It was only in the afternoon of that memorable day, when the nervous excitement of the event had worn off, that I experienced a feeling of weariness such as I have never known before or since.

A great part of my speech was devoted to proving how completely mistaken were the territorial clauses of the Treaty of Trianon from an ethnographical standpoint. It showed how some of the proposals were a direct blow in the face for the principle of nationality which was their slogan. While I was explaining this in English, Lloyd George sent a note to Clemenceau, which the latter was obviously annoyed to receive, though he answered it by a nod of the head to Lloyd George. I was curious as to what this incident meant, and I was not informed until my speech was over. When I had finished, Clemenceau called on Lloyd George to speak, and the latter invited me to supply more detailed explanations of what I had said in the course of my speech concerning the distribution of races, and especially of the Magyars, in the territories detached from Hungary.

I now understood why Clemenceau had seemed put out

when Lloyd George's note was handed to him. The principle by which no discussion should be allowed had been broken to some extent by this request for more exact explanations. Fortunately, I was prepared for such questions. I had brought with me Pál Teleki's excellent ethnographical map of Hungary, and with this I went up to where Lloyd George was sitting. The national leaders crowded there in a body, and with their heads together over a map heard my explanations. These obviously caused them to have some doubts about the wisdom of the vivisection which they had proposed to carry out on my poor country without sufficient anatomical knowledge. Lloyd George whispered to me, "You were very eloquent." I replied, "If there was any eloquence, it was not mine, but the eloquence of facts."

I was told, in fact, that after this meeting some quite strong protests were made by England and Italy, who complained that they had been led into the unpleasant situation of being made a party to such gross errors. Nitti even made a serious attempt to bring about certain changes in the more absurd clauses of the treaty, but he was at length overruled by the argument that the entire map arranged by their peace treaties would collapse if an alteration were permitted in any part.

When I had come safely to the end of my French and English addresses, and, out of politeness, had spoken a few words to the Italian delegation in their own language,

Clemenceau made me a little speech, whose almost friendly tone was in striking contrast to that which he had adopted at the beginning of the meeting.

"Monsieur le Président,"—he said in effect—"you have seen with what keen attention the whole Supreme Council has followed your statements. You will certainly not expect that we should at once make up our minds about what you have told us. You may rest assured, however, that we will give the most careful and close consideration to this matter. Meanwhile, we are awaiting the written answer of the Hungarian delegation to the terms of peace which have been submitted to them, and we would ask you to tell us how long you will require to complete your reply." I asked for an interval of four weeks, which was immediately granted.

And so ended the morning which had brought me the most difficult hours of my public life.

There can be no doubt that, on the whole, a somewhat more favourable atmosphere was created among those with whom the decision rested. It was clearly perceptible wherever we had direct contact with Allied circles. On the other hand, there was no sign of it in the Paris press. The reports which appeared there on the meeting I have described were obviously from an official source. In these, some tribute was paid to my linguistic achievement, while the truth of my statements was brushed aside with a few derisive observations of a general kind.

No words need be wasted in explaining why the French press was hostile to our mission, for this hostility was a natural consequence of the situation. How carefully this hostile attitude had been worked up may be seen from the following almost incredible details. Thirteen years earlier, in 1907, on the occasion of an Inter-Parliamentary meeting held in Berlin, I had delivered a humorous speech at a dinner-party. In the course of this, I remarked that, if the man in the moon came down for a short time to the earth and asked me which of our so-called world languages he should learn for the sake of his general education, I would unquestionably recommend German, because the assimilative power of the German intellect would open the way for him through excellent translations to the greatest number of cultural achievements in other lands. This was brought up against me in the Paris press—I repeat, after thirteen years—as a proof of excessive pro-German feeling! Still more amazing was a reference in the Paris press to an equally humorous after-dinner speech which I had made in Budapest many years before the outbreak of war, in honour of Dr. Gyula Vargha, then head of the Bureau of Statistics. On the occasion of some jubilee or other, his friends arranged an agreeable little dinner-party, at which I remarked that Vargha, who was also a lyrical poet of some standing, would be capable of transfiguring even the driest figures into poetry by the ardour of his patriotism. I had completely forgotten about this speech, and was astounded to see it reprinted by the Paris press in 1920 as evidence that Hungarian statistics were no more than poetical falsification. This resuscitation of long-forgotten remarks, which even in their time had had no significance, typifies the atmosphere in which we lived.

For the moment, we had nothing further to do in France. The detailed statement in which we were to reply to the terms of peace that had been handed us could be prepared just as well, and even better, in Budapest than in Paris. After a stay of ten days, we therefore set out for home on January 18.

In Budapest we were received, on our arrival at the station, by all the members of the government, as well as by Admiral Horthy, who was not yet Regent, but Commander-in-Chief of the Hungarian forces, and an immense crowd of people. The entire city had been decked out with black flags on receiving official news of the terms of peace. In the addresses of welcome one felt, besides their warm acknowledgment of our efforts, a painful sense of hopelessness, which was only the logical reaction after the mood of unwarranted confidence that they had felt a short time before. It was our duty now to protest against this other extreme, and, in my reply to the official welcome, I asked the authorities to have these black flags removed, and to support the work of the peace delegation, which was only now entering upon its decisive stage, by preserving their self-control like men.

We began our work immediately. The situation was thrashed out with eminent politicians of all parties, and, with the assistance of leading experts in all branches of public life, a complete, detailed statement was prepared of the injustices and shortcomings in the draft treaty. On February 12, we returned to Paris, and, on our arrival, at once handed over our voluminous answer to the Supreme Council. Once this had been accomplished, we had nothing further to do but to wait in Neuilly for the final decision which the Supreme Council would make, after they had considered our reply.

We waited until March 31.

The events of that month and a half belong to the preliminary history of the Treaty of Trianon, and are to a great extent still unsuitable for publication. Here I intend to speak only of matters which can be treated in an anecdotal way, and which throw some light on the psychological situation.

As I have said, the Hungarian peace delegation had returned to Paris, or more correctly to Neuilly, provided with an immense amount of material which had been worked up for them on ethnography, geography, history, finance, trade, hydrography and other technical subjects. We occupied our place of internment again, under the same conditions as during our first stay. All contact with Paris was forbidden. It happened once that a French lady, who had been governess in the house of one of our delegates—Vilmos Lers, State Secretary in the Ministry of Trade—and was now living with her children in Paris, read in the newspaper the name which she knew so well. She came to Neuilly to welcome the father of her former pupils, but she was not allowed to see him. This is only one instance to show how inflexibly the principle of our isolation from the outer world was maintained. After the short interval of relief which we experienced when the general atmosphere had seemed brighter, we relapsed into the dark pessimism which we had brought with us on our first arrival in Paris. This was increased by the inactivity which our situation forced upon us. We had nothing to do but to wait and see what decision we would receive concerning the critical statement we had handed in. We could not even hope that we might soon be enlightened on this point, but on the contrary were obliged to look upon this postponement of the answer as a good sign, for it allowed us to assume that the arguments we had advanced were being made the subject of serious discussion. In daily consultations, we racked our brains to know what we might still do for the advancement of our cause. We made use of every possible occasion to address notes on this or that special point to the Supreme Council, in most cases without receiving an answer. An exception to this was one lengthy memorandum which I personally addressed to the newly-elected President of the Republic, Monsieur Deschanel, with whom I had formerly been on very good terms, in which I endeavoured to make clear certain consequences of the partition of Hungary which would affect the special interests of France. This memorandum was at least thought worthy of an acknowledgment.

From a human point of view, another incident is perhaps not without interest, as it is certainly gratifying. I received private information that one of my oldest friends, who was living at Temesvar—a town seized by the Rumanians—was the victim of particularly virulent persecution which might even lead to his being sentenced by a military court. I wrote personally to Clemenceau appealing to his humanity, in the hope that he would intervene on my friend's behalf. I received no answer, but I assume the intervention took place, because the persecution suddenly ceased.

Some members of our delegation who had friends in Paris got in touch with them by letter, and arranged to meet them at certain parts of the Bois de Boulogne. They were not a little proud of having thus broken through the internment cordon, although these secret meetings could be of no great help, except in so far as they gave us more information about events in French politics than we could derive from the newspapers. I would add that these skilfully plotted meetings of conspirators ended humorously. At the end of March, when our duties in Paris were over, we returned definitely to Budapest, leaving only Mr. Prasnowsky, afterwards Hungarian Minister in Paris, to settle any remaining details. One day our chief military supervisor, the same Colonel Henry whom I have already mentioned, came and smilingly handed him a sheet of paper with these words: "You will find here, my dear Monsieur Prasnowsky, a list of all the people whom you have met in the Bois de Boulogne. I am not criticising you, far from it. But I would not like you to think us fools." We had therefore been under much closer observation than we had suspected.

Great was our surprise when one day two countrymen of ours living in Paris, Dr. Károly Halmos and Andor Semsey, who afterwards entered the Hungarian diplomatic service, were led into our conference room by Colonel Henry, and we were informed that these gentlemen had free access to us at any time. What could have happened? In high French financial circles, a movement had started for a large scale trade agreement with Hungary. That this was considered very seriously is proved by the fact that the firm of Schneider-Creusot was taking the lead. This firm enjoyed the favour of influential political circles in France, and met with such support at the Quai d'Orsay that, at their request, the gates of our internment house were opened. Mr. Halmos had business connections with these financial circles, and it was taken for granted that they would use all their influence to secure a modification of the conditions of peace imposed upon Hungary.

From now on, our presence within the radius of Paris acquired an entirely new character. Members of our delegation could often go to Paris, and even deal directly with the Quai d'Orsay. I designated for this purpose, with the subsequent approval of the Government, Count Imre Csáky, and afterwards, on the advice of our financial experts, Counts István Bethlen and Pál Teleki. I thought it best not to take part myself in the negotiations. They lasted well on into the summer, long after the Hungarian peace delegation had ceased to exist. It does not belong to these recollections to describe the hopes which they aroused, or the reason why they came to nothing. Throughout most of our second stay, they created for us a better, and almost hopeful, atmosphere, which we breathed as eagerly as a man breathes the pure air when he comes suddenly into the open from some stuffy room. I well remember how we won back our sense of humour, and how certain members of the delegation went into Paris to hear some of the frequent concerts of the season, without being prevented by the authorities. The inevitable detective travelled with them to a certain point in the city, where our friends were given complete liberty of movement until the hour arranged for their return to Neuilly.

I myself only made use of this chance to visit the city under police supervision when an acute toothache made it necessary. This happened in the early part of our stay, perhaps about the beginning of March. The detective travelled with me to the dentist, and remained in the waiting room until I had been treated, when he again took me under his protection. As it was then almost spring, and I had only brought with me a warm winter overcoat, I availed myself of one of these dental expeditions to buy a spring coat in one of the big Paris shops, I think the Bon Marché. The detective of course accompanied me there, and he could not rest until he had whispered my identity right and left to the entire personnel of the departments we crossed. The consequence was that, on reaching the overcoat department, I was surrounded by a whole group of inquisitive people, who obviously wanted to see if a Boche looked human and had civilised manners. This flattering curiosity was not to the advantage of my business transaction. It caused me to finish it as quickly as possible, and the result was that I came to possess an overcoat which did not suit me at all. I gave it the name of the Danaïd coat, because, instead of the pocket in which I usually carry my handkerchief, it had only an opening, whose purpose was not made clear, on either side, through which I lost many handkerchiefs, before I got used to the situation. This overcoat, and the losses which it caused me, were the subject of much merriment in our delegation, and it remained the only material souvenir which I carried away with me from this otherwise very serious visit. Seen from that point of view, my acquisition of it is an example of the frequent mingling of the grotesque with the serious, or even tragic, of which anyone who has been through serious events in his life can relate instances.

We left Paris at the end of March, because the negotiations which were taking place did not require the presence of our whole delegation and had also to be carried on partly in Budapest. We were in a comparatively joyful frame of mind. The answer of the Allied Powers to our observations on the proposed treaty had not been received at the time of our departure. It had been postponed until it was known if, how far and in what manner the peace treaty might be modified as a result of the negotiations, though these were admittedly only of a business kind. The Hungarian government never concealed the fact that they could only make business concessions in return for others of a political nature.

It will make an interesting chapter in the history of our times when it is possible to describe why and when the whole attempt finally collapsed.

When this failure had once been ascertained, there was nothing left for it but to accept the fate which was ordained for us. The day at last broke on which was held that tragic session of Parliament at which the Treaty of Trianon was to be ratified. No one who took part in this ceremony in Parliament will ever forget it. The dry, business-like way in which the event was carried out heightened its terrible effectiveness. A minority protested against the ratification, and left the chamber. The majority stayed behind, and remained silent when the President asked if the assembly agreed to ratification. Thereupon, the President assumed that no opposition was being made, and hence that the ratification must be taken as voted. Under the impulse of an irresistible instinct, the whole assembly rose and broke out into the Hungarian national anthem, the voices of the gallery mingling with those of the members. No eye remained dry. Since that day, the flags on the Parliament House and on all other public buildings are flown continually at half-mast.

Thus was the seal set upon the vanity of our efforts. It redounds greatly to the honour of my people that they have borne no grudge against the members of the peace delegation, and in particular against me, its leader, for the failure we incurred but, on the contrary, have valued our valiant attempt as highly as if success had crowned it. This nation has indeed its faults, but meanness of disposition is not among them. It is noble and generous through and through in its sentiments. I would almost say that its soul is too great for the wasted body into which it has been crushed, though it gives to that body a power of achievement far greater than its population would seem to support. To have served this nation faithfully, as I believe, for sixty years, and perhaps to be able to serve her longer, is my pride and joy in the evening of my life.

My first visit to Paris after the events which I have here described took place the following year. The atmosphere

which I found there was so similar to the one I had known
as leader of the peace delegation that it may still be
described in this chapter under the heading of "How
Peace was made after the Great War." I use the word
"atmosphere" because all external circumstances which
would have indicated a continuance of the state of war,
such as, for example, the limitation of one's freedom of
movement and so on, had, of course, disappeared. Immediately after the signing of the Treaty of Trianon, we
had shaken hands, and this was now permitted to everyone, but not everyone took to it kindly, as I was soon to
discover. I had come to Paris to take part in a meeting of
the League of Nations Union, which was then being
formed, and from which we could not absent ourselves.
I made use of the opportunity to get in touch with some
leading politicians, which I was easily able to do. The most
interesting conversations I had were with the new President of the Republic, Alexandre Millerand, and with
Monsieur Poincaré, who was then looked upon as the
head of the extreme nationalists. I also called on Palé-
ologue's successor, Berthelot, who was the actual head of
French foreign policy, and not so well disposed towards us
as his predecessor. The welcome I received from him was
most courteous, but the conversations which I had with
him were calculated to destroy any illusions I might still
be cherishing. He was always stressing the fact that the
peace treaties which had just been signed must never be

altered, and that Hungary would have to reconcile herself to this situation. This was no surprise to me, and for that reason I was not greatly impressed. It was Raymond Poincaré who spoke out more clearly than any. The conversation with him lasted for about an hour, and as he had no official post at the moment, he put off his reserve and allowed me to have a frank conversation on all matters. We carried on a discussion about the problem of war guilt, and our talk terminated in a sentence which he delivered with his customary sharp intonation. I remember it word for word. "The whole question comes to this: Is Hungary definitely prepared to accept the situation made for her by the Treaty, without any intention of bringing about a change? If so, we can get on very well together." As he was obviously waiting for an answer, I spoke as follows,—I can quote my reply almost word for word: "Monsieur Poincaré, am I to tell you a lie? In that case, you would not believe me, so I will answer 'No.' Hungary cannot accept the injustice which has been inflicted on her. One thing of which I am certain, though, is that we are not thinking of violent methods to restore our rights." Poincaré's reply was not quite audible, but I thought I heard something like "It's always like that." With this, I took my leave of a statesman for whom I have the greatest respect, in spite of his rough manner. These semi-official conversations were quite calm and orderly. I was still looked upon as the President of the Hungarian peace delegation, and therefore a person who enjoyed to some extent diplomatic immunity.

Of quite another kind was my first meeting with unofficial people who took part, like myself, in the sessions of the League of Nations Union. Some of these I had met more than once in the course of the year at Inter-Parliamentary Conferences, and I was on friendly terms with them. Chief among these was the late Senator, d'Estournelles de Constant, who had been my guest at Eberhard, and who had given me the warmest welcome whenever I came to Paris in the last years before the War. At his hospitable house, he had always arranged for me to meet such politicians as I was particularly interested in. All unsuspecting, I went up to him and offered my hand, but his attitude was icy. Reluctantly and with a bad grace, he accepted my handshake, and, in answer to my friendly words, said just as much as was necessary in order not to be actually rude. I saw quite clearly how another of my old friends manœuvred to avoid meeting me, which made me feel very uncomfortable. On the same afternoon d'Estournelles de Constant felt obliged to offer an explanation. It was clear that it hurt this good and kind man to be forced, as he thought, to adopt this attitude with an old friend. He came up to me, and said that he felt he owed it to our former friendship to explain the distant manner which he must now assume towards me.

284

It was his duty to behave in this way, because I had been one of those who caused the War and among the most eager promoters of it. To this amazing accusation I could only retort: "As regards the origin of the War, I can prove an alibi, for when the ultimatum was sent to Serbia I was on the coast of Belgium, the very last place where I would have chosen to be if I had had any idea of what was going to happen. As regards my having urged the continuance of the War, I do not hesitate to admit that, once the die was cast and the clash could not be avoided, I put forth all my efforts, in word and writing, at home and abroad, to sustain the energy and enthusiasm of my people in their decisive struggle."

I do not know if d'Estournelles regarded this attitude as an incitement to war, but I do know that, had he been in the same position, he would have behaved as I did. D'Estournelles was obviously touched, but he did not submit at once and it was not for me to take any further steps towards reconciliation. This was to happen at our next meeting, in the course of a Council session of the Inter-Parliamentary Union, when he overwhelmed me with signs of esteem and friendship. Whenever an opportunity presented itself, he tried to support my suggestions and, in fact, to make up for the rudeness of his behaviour at our first meeting, without actually having to offer an explanation. I willingly responded

285

to this method of silent compromise, but I knew all the time how deeply embedded was the war psychosis, and I realised the necessity, both from a political and from a personal point of view, of re-establishing our former contacts . . .

I have thought it worth while to record these personal memories because they throw considerable light on the war psychology which was still uppermost when the treaties were signed in 1919–20, and thus enable one to understand the nature of that peace-making. At the same time, I wish to put on record that I have been able in subsequent years to observe the progressive subsidence of these emotional antagonisms. This has been clear to me at various international assemblies, such as Inter-Parliamentary Conferences, meetings of the League of Nations Union, and the periodical sessions of the League of Nations itself which I have attended regularly for eight years as the representative of my country. I am prepared to state my opinion that the political differences which are still outstanding will no longer be embittered by enmities of a personal kind. Ties have been established which should assist the peaceful settlement of difficulties that are objective in character. Whatever may be said against the League of Nations —and I do not deny that its activities leave much to be desired—the opportunity which it provides for international discussion is a service of incalculable importance to the cause of international reconciliation.

However great the antagonisms and difficulties may still be, I hope that a continuation of this chapter will appear within a reasonable time under the title of "How real peace was made in the year *x*."

CHAPTER VIII

THE CRISIS IN THE LEAGUE OF NATIONS

It is generally recognised that the League of Nations is passing through a severe crisis, which challenges its moral authority and therefore its very existence. No one can deny that this is true, but the manner in which the fact is admitted differs greatly according to one's preconceived opinions. Those who do not believe in the possibility, or at any rate the practicability, of international organisations to secure peace, and who have therefore rejected on principle all idea of a League of Nations, see their opinion confirmed by the course of events, and many of them can hardly conceal the malicious joy which this causes them. There are some people, however, who believe in the necessity for mankind to progress in such a way that the spirit and letter of co-operation will replace our old struggle for supremacy. These people have taken to the idea of the League of Nations, because it offers an instrument to effect this progress, though they do not lose sight of the difficulties by which so complete a reorganisation of the world is necessarily attended. They regard the crisis which threatens this first attempt to give it concrete form with regret, but at the same time with the wish and the hope that it may be overcome, and that valuable lessons may be learnt from it.

I need hardly say that I belong to this second category, and can only discuss the subject from that standpoint.

The present crisis in the League of Nations is to be seen in three great problems, with regard to which the League has not yet succeeded in carrying out what was expected of it. These three are the great Far Eastern dispute, the world trade depression, and general disarmament.

I would like in a few words to trace the connection between each of these problems and the League, what might, in fact, be called the relative scale of their significance for it, as well as the present position with regard to each. The dispute in the Far East is an incidental matter, such as may crop up at any time, though admittedly in this case a very weighty and difficult one. It is greatly to the credit of the League if it succeeds in settling such disputes, but it is no reflection on the merit of the League if it fails in a case where virtually cosmic forces are in collision. It would be as if the reputation of a hospital or a great doctor were to collapse upon their failure to save some desperately sick man. What we can unquestionably ask of the League and of the doctor is that they should conscientiously apply all remedies at their disposal.

This is equally true of the League and the world trade depression. Judgment must be founded on what it has put forward in the way of advice, and of the mediation and assistance which it has offered. It cannot be made responsible for the folly of certain States which refuse its lead, and for the evil consequences of such folly.

Of a very different kind is the connection between the League and the disarmament problem, whose solution is referred to in the Covenant itself as a vital matter, the lines on which this solution should proceed being actually stated there. This is an internal, organic problem of the League which it is morally bound to solve, in accordance with the principles of Article 8 of the Covenant. Success or failure in this problem means life or death for the League of Nations. It is very gratifying to observe that the prospects of success have been substantially improved by the decision of the five Great Powers to recognise the principle of equality for all States, in this as in other questions. Only those who are prejudiced can now say that the League has failed in this sphere of its duties, even though the obstacles which beset the realisation of this principle are still to be overcome.

I intend to discuss in some detail the organic defects of the League, having regard to our present stage of world evolution. Most of the difficulties encountered in individual cases arise out of them. The introductory Article of the League Covenant calls upon it to secure justice, honour and respect for rights in the relations between peoples, and thus to set peace on a firm and permanent footing. With this object, the separate Articles of the Covenant assign powers to the organs of the League—Assembly and Council—by which they can pronounce certain judgments in international controversies. In cases where the conflict depends upon a legal dispute, a judicial decision is provided for, but the organs of the League have to see that these decisions are carried out. There are also individual legal disputes, such as those connected with the agreements for protecting minorities, in which the Council of the League has to pronounce judgment. The aim of these judgments is always to carry out the introductory Article of the Covenant, namely, to secure justice, honour, and the respect for rights in international dealings. Everything must be subordinated to the common interests of humanity, for it is only by this means that a lasting peace can be secured.

The question now arises as to how far the composition of the organs of the League is adequate to this task, and we can only reply that it is very far from being so. For it to be otherwise, the community of nations would have to control organs which belonged to it alone, and knew no other interest than theirs. Such organs do not exist, nor will they ever until the inhabitants of Mars have been induced to collaborate. In this world, even for the League of Nations there can be no other organs than the representatives of individual nations. However much these may be filled with the spirit of human co-operation, they remain representatives of their own people, and can neither escape from their mental world nor renounce the desire to serve their interests. It is therefore inevitable that these special interests exercise the greatest influence on the attitude taken up by League delegates in dealing with international questions. We are not here concerned with a conscious violation of duty on the part of these delegates, for one unconsciously sees collective interests from the standpoint of the special interests of one's own country. Should one perceive a clash between these two kinds of interests in any one instance, the overwhelming majority of men to-day look upon it as their duty to put the interests of their own country before those of others. The same men who indignantly repudiate the suggestion that they would sacrifice the interests of justice or of their country to their own private advantage, think it quite natural to put the interests of their country above those of mankind as a whole. Selfishness, which is regarded as a vice in individuals, becomes a "sacred egoism" in the eyes of the vast majority when thinking of their native land.

Since this attitude is the prevailing one, the part taken by representatives of different nations in the League is still largely influenced by the effort to find in that institution another means of advancing their own national interests.

This opposition between the idea of the League and the attitude of the men who compose it is modified by the fact that any claims of individual nations at the League can only be conceded with the help of representatives from other countries, and therefore conformably to their own claims and interests. Here we have certainly the grossest form of altruism, namely, far-sighted selfishness. Even this leads, nevertheless, to a kind of balance of interests, in which admittedly the strong are still supreme, and the League, as at present constituted, has become a political instrument in the hands of the mightiest among the mighty. These have to reckon with the remaining nations to some extent, but in the end they always carry their point. The mightiest among the mighty are those Powers whose influence over the smaller States is the most far-reaching, for the judicial equality of nations in the League is a delusion. Every little State will need to think very carefully before opposing, especially in some matter which does not directly concern it, a Great Power whose shadow falls across its whole life.

What follows from these observations which will appear justified to everyone who wishes to look facts in the face? Is one to renounce the idea of a League representing great collective interests, as its Covenant declares, or are we to shut our eyes, or at least our mouths, to unpleasant facts, and go on living in a world of illusions?

We must do neither of these. We should draw the simple conclusion that the League of Nations is still in a process of development, and that we can therefore expect no more from it than the stage which it has reached in its evolution allows us. Admittedly, it will always be difficult for those who belong to one nation to be at the same time representatives of the whole. This difficulty, however, will constantly diminish, and in the end will become a factor whose influence will hardly ever be felt. This will happen just as quickly as the patriotic idea undergoes modification, which will be brought about, not by any new ideology, but by the facts of world progress. In past centuries national feeling was governed by the ideology of imperialism; in other words, by the effort to raise oneself above other nations, forcing these into a position of inferiority compared to one's own, and endeavouring to make one's nation sovereign within a certain sphere. From an ethical point of view, this was a very questionable form of patriotism, but it was admissible then. To-day it is no longer so. In our time, no nation can enrich itself by destroying another. The world economic crisis with which we are struggling makes that consideration plain to all. The recognition of this has come earlier in the economic field, where palpable facts, which can be expressed in figures, tell their tale, than in the departments of morality and politics. The same forces which make isolation of interests impossible are active there also, though their effects are slower and take on a less obvious form.

Imperialistic patriotism endeavoured to secure for one people a brilliant, but perilous, position, which was always threatened by changing destiny, so that at any moment the nation which had reached the height of what it called greatness might be hurled into the abyss. The greatness which imperialism brought to countries was unstable, and the statesman who led his people along that road might be compared to a father who proposes to secure the future of his family by reckless speculation. Human common sense, the experience of the Great War and its ever-changing consequences have all gone to prove as clearly as possible that this kind of policy is fundamental madness. As a contrast, they show us that leading statesmen should follow the example of those other fathers who prefer solid investments, bringing in a modest, but safe, income, to speculations that lead to the brink of ruin. It is clear that our duty is to give security to a nation even more perhaps than to a family, for this alone can serve as a basis upon which all the resources and potentialities of the nation can be developed. This reasonable kind of patriotism is most certainly not inferior in a moral sense to the unreasonable. Its predominance will induce the nations and their leading statesmen more and more to seek their welfare, their honour, their progress, and the security of their rights in a policy based on the condition of peace with other countries, and of the recognition by all of everything which is vitally important to any one of them. That is no Utopia, but sound common sense. It is the natural development of a feeling which will, and should, never die out, namely, the love of one's own people, directed by reason towards a compromise with another force, which is becoming ever more real—the collective welfare of human society as a whole. The nations will eventually weary of seeing their real interests sacrificed to antagonisms which they do not really feel, and whose embitterment brings satisfaction only to a few prominent men, and never to the mass of the people.

The future of the League will depend upon the course which this evolution follows.

To-day we are only at the beginning. Moreover, there are many obstacles in the way. I would almost say that the League of Nations has been born prematurely. It was created at a time when the state of mind which should control it was not yet matured. The imperialist way of thinking was just in the act of celebrating its wildest orgies. Reinforced by its atavistic appeal, it had burst into delirium in the terrible explosion of the Great War. Not only was it given legal form in the peace treaties, but it received a lasting encouragement from those clauses which seek to perpetuate the inequalities between victors and vanquished. If we try to express the difficulties with which the League has to contend in one sentence, we must say that they depend on the following fact: the outer form of the League was made before the spirit was ready to occupy it. Since, however, it has been formed in this way, our only duty is to bring that spirit into being as quickly and completely as possible, by overcoming all the obstacles to its development. The existing form of the League can help us in many ways to accomplish this difficult task, and especially through those two instruments of progress which we find in its own activity—the periodical meeting of representatives of all nations, and the publicity it offers.

I can speak from personal knowledge concerning the effectiveness of both. In frank conversations between the representatives of different ways of thinking, a kind of agreement springs up in the course of the years, a mutual understanding which would be otherwise quite impossible. It would be a crass and wilful pessimism to overlook the progress which certain ideas have made as year after year goes by, especially those which interest us, as the losers in the Great War. Who dared mention, for example, only a few years ago, the word "Revision" in good society—I mean in what our war-time opponents would call good society? To-day it is on everyone's lips, and the rapid increase in the number of those who believe that this most difficult among all the tasks of reconstruction is unavoidable, gathers speed from day to day. It is not only leading statesmen for whom the meetings of the League offer a constantly recurring opportunity of personal discussion, without the sensational background of official visits. The more modest factors in international politics, who, quite insensibly, prepare the way for public opinion in all countries, meet at the League, where they can talk over matters without engaging themselves, and experience, whether they wish it or not, the modification in their own way of thought which a meeting with other opinions always produces. As to publicity, this has set bounds, at any rate in Europe, to the worst outbreaks of imperialism. We have at least progressed so far that imperialism is inclined to be ashamed of itself, rather than to boast, and it depends only upon the courage of those who speak from the platform of the League of Nations to hinder its efforts. It is our special duty, as representatives of the vanquished States, gradually to overcome the delay in establishing equality among the nations, which still persists to our disadvantage. This we can do by a consistent, calm, and courageous bearing.

My purpose in drawing attention to the deeper reasons for this lack of equality has been to make clear that the existence of these reasons now is as inevitable as their gradual disappearance will be in the course of human progress. It would therefore be quite a mistake to let the dissatisfaction which we all feel in this matter grow into hostility and mistrust for the idea of the League. Weak as we are, we require the League of Nations, if anyone does: not as it is, but as it should and will be, if we consistently carry out our duty.

When we study the growth of the League without prejudice, we cannot deny that, as regards the cure of its organic defects, much has been achieved, while positive results as well are to be recorded. The League created the permanent Court of International Justice at The Hague, in whose atmosphere such success has been obtained that nearly all States have bound themselves by treaty to bring legal disputes before this Court, or before a Court of Arbitration. It was at the League of Nations that there originated an *acte général* codifying the obligation of countries to settle non-legal disputes by mediation. Thanks to this, the effectiveness of the Kellogg Pact was first secured, and the universal acceptance of this Pact was also an achievement of the League. The *acte général* has not yet been accepted by all countries, but it is to be hoped that this will soon be the case, perhaps with the help of some modifications in the text. Who would claim that the points I have here enumerated are of no importance for the preservation of peace? Who can deny, therefore, that the League by which all this has been made possible has performed a great service to the cause of peace, even in its present far from perfect form? If only we can succeed in finding a just solution, acceptable to all nations, of the disarmament problem, in which 1933 has much better prospects than the previous year, we will be able to say that, when accounts are drawn up impartially, the credit side of the League will outweigh the debit. This will be still more the case if we count in, as is only fair, that progress towards a change in the thought of mankind which I have already indicated.

It has to be admitted that across this picture looms the dark cloud of war in the Far East and of the failure, perhaps even the inefficiency, of the action taken by the League with regard to this problem. It is natural that opinion at large should be dominated by this weighty and sensational episode. Here I must once more refer back to what I have said already. Failure in such a collision of elemental forces would not in itself justify a hostile verdict on the institution of the League, provided this takes up an attitude corresponding to the principles on which it is founded. This must be the concern of those Powers in whose hands the decision chiefly rests, rightly enough in this case, for they are much more closely interested in the problem than smaller countries like ourselves.

I have reached the end of my observations. The conclusion I draw from them is that we do not despair of the future of the League because of certain isolated impressions; in fact, that we have not even the right to doubt it. My view is that the representatives of all countries, especially those of the States beaten in the

Great War, must work on the lines of a calm, deliberate and bold co-operation to do away with the defects which still weaken it, but which, as is my firm conviction, will gradually disappear.

Once more: I believe in the League of Nations, not as it is, but as it will be.

CHAPTER IX

ON OLD AGE

THIS is a subject upon which I can claim, without immodesty, that I am entitled to speak. Am I—or let us put it in a more general way—is one still competent at my age of eighty-seven years to observe the things of the past in the light of the present and the future, by which alone they take on their true colours? Does the inevitable weakening of one's organism which sets in with advancing years extend to all one's faculties, and in what degree? Are there compensating advantages in old age, thanks to which this phase may be regarded as a factor of independent value in the life of mankind?

To all these questions there can obviously be no general answer, or at least we can only offer one with the same reservations and limiting conditions which we must make when speaking of youth in general. There are different kinds of old age, just as there are different kinds of youth. In both phases of personal evolution, the individual is as significant as the type. I will endeavour to combine both, though as a starting point I can only take my personal experience and my own old age.

I shall be dealing with an old age which has only made itself felt, as regards physical decay, from my eightieth year onwards, though even since then it has been spared sickness and pain. I realised this physical weakening when I stopped for a few days at Taormina on my way back from Egypt. Three years previously, I had spent a few weeks at that enchanting spot, and had then done excursions into the mountains without effort, though they included some steep climbing over wild country. That was no longer possible. This time, I sought out regular paths, and wherever any extra strain was put upon my muscles in order to keep my balance, it was somewhat disagreeable. That was about all I noticed.

To a man in whose life mental work has always played a greater part than sport, or bodily exercise, this is of no great significance, for those faculties have not failed me by whose help we know the pleasures of the mind, the stimulation of great art and especially the deepening of one's experience by music, which has filled, and fills to-day, so great a place in my mental life. One could even say that these impressions have become more vivid in proportion as external activity has diminished.

Let us, therefore, consider exclusively the life of the mind, and let us examine its activity at this final stage. Does it deteriorate in every respect? Is it any longer of value, and can it still achieve useful results?

Here again, a universally valid answer is impossible. The individual case is decisive, and the individual as a witness of his own experience can merely testify to this. Judgment as to the objective significance of his statement must be left to others.

With this reservation, I would say that I perceive no weakening of the power to take in, understand and express accurately even new ideas. I would almost say that clarity and the power to survey and classify wide domains of thought have increased. Continued mental activity of any kind brings, not weariness, but animation, which I feel in a keener sense of well-being. This refers especially to philosophical meditations, which throughout my life have acted as a kind of intellectual change of air for the poor professional politician I have always been, a health treatment like that of the townsman, when he goes to stay at the seaside or in the Alps. In them, I have always found a means of increasing the clarity and breadth of vision which I could bring to my work. The hearing of great music has had a similar effect on me. If I were anticipating some great mental effort, as on the eve of a big Parliamentary battle, I could best prepare myself by listening to a Beethoven symphony. With its help, I would gain more breadth of view than if I had worked mentally for days. Music I would call meta-metaphysics, for its realm begins where the spoken word, and even the word as thought conceives it, stops short. It is as important to me now as ever before, if not more so. Never, throughout my whole life, has this flight of the spirit to higher regions been easier and more fruitful than now, in my old age. This is due perhaps to the gradual renunciation of self which is a consequence of the decline in physical vitality. We feel nearer to life as a whole, and the spiritual force which unites us with it acquires an ever-increasing strength. That may be only relative—I do not venture to judge—but, in any case, it offers a rich substitute for what we have lost.

So much for the intellectual side of old age in general. What are we to say of its attitude to the problems of practical life, especially to political and social questions? Here we touch upon a subject beset with complications and individual differences whose common elements I would assemble in the question: What is the old man's attitude towards the movements and changes in all things which he has witnessed? Can he understand them? Can he reconcile himself to them? Can he take an active part in their progress?

Some are able to do this, while others cannot, and this is the real dividing line between old men who preserve the fullness of life and those who are more like a living memory.

These last are perhaps the rule. In his fine study of the different phases of life, Horace has drawn the old man— *Laudator temporis acti se puero*—praising the times in which he was young. An old man of this type cannot, or will not, understand that everything changes, and that conditions of life take on other forms. He considers everything new to be bad, and tries, at least in his own person, to hold back, entrenching himself behind old habits and ideas. In a retrospective way, he may still remain of intellectual significance and be an interesting object for study. So long as he does not feel the touch of the modernity which he hates, he may be friendly and attractive, but he has ceased to develop, and therefore to live.

The other type of old man is the one who understands. This type again breaks up into a number of distinct nuances, which I would assemble in two sub-groups. To the first belong those who realise the inevitability of change, but look upon it as an evil which they regret. To the second belong those who are "in the swing," that is to say, who take part in new movements. They do so without the conviction of infallibility and the dogmatic habits which belong to youth, in a spirit of benevolent criticism that bestows a high value upon their assistance. They regard, moreover, in the same spirit of criticism that which is their own personal province, namely, experience. This latter demands criticism no less than does abstract thought, for the so-called wisdom of experience is just as inclined as abstract theorising to degenerate into doctrinaire statements. We believe readily that the same causes always lead to the same results, without taking into account all the attendant circumstances which influence those results, and may affect them in a different way at different times. The application of experience to practice therefore demands as much care and skill as the application of theory. Ability to use experience in this way as an instrument of knowledge, instead of becoming its slave, is peculiar to the old man who can help in building a bridge between past and future. Others may have to undertake the active work, but his advice will always be listened to with advantage.

How comes it that certain old men preserve the fullness of life, and can still follow a useful calling? At this point, I may perhaps be allowed to seek for an explanation in my own case, for I believe myself to be one of this type of the active aged. I love my own times, without being blind to their unhappy errors. I think I understand the laws which govern their development, and I take part in progress with an eagerness which is not diminished by the keen critical faculty that experience brings. What is the actual reason for this? In answering that question, we will leave out of account the minor forces which affect a man's mental disposition in individual cases, such as good or bad health, favourable or unfavourable conditions of life, and so on, however decisive such circumstances may often be. We will consider the problem exclusively from the organic side, and establish a general rule governing the capacity or non-capacity in old age of reconciling oneself to what is new. The following explanation, which I take from my own experience, seems to me the most plausible.

If, as is actually the case, I have no difficulty in coming to terms with the social evolution now taking place, and am willing to collaborate in it, the reason is probably that my thoughts as a young man tended in that direction. For me, therefore, this evolution marks no new turn of events with which I have perforce to reconcile myself from now onwards, but the approach towards a goal which I have had in mind since I first turned towards it in my youth. This goal was that of social equality in everything which is fundamental to human dignity and to the requirements of human happiness. I am not proposing artificial barriers to the development of inborn moral and mental superiority and of the inequalities arising out of these, for that would mean disaster to our race. I am thinking of a state of things which would assure to everyone an existence worthy of man, and would offer to all the same conditions for the development of their gifts. At the beginning of my economic studies, which I pursued in the hey-day of the so-called classical Political Economy, long before sociology made its appearance, I revolted against the mastery of material things over human beings, always assumed by the economists, who put forward as their supreme goal the greatest possible production of goods, rather than the most widespread human happiness. It was

Count Apponyi with his family

believed that this last condition would result logically from the other, but this has proved to be an illusion. It was repugnant to me to see wages, which determined the economic fate of millions of our fellow-men, discussed chiefly among the costs of production, and hence to see low wages, with the resulting low standard of life of the working masses, reckoned an advantage in international competition. As a contrast to all this, I determined, from the earliest phase of my thinking on economics and sociology, to set man once more on his rightful throne, as the real object of all economic activity, and I thought not only of a few privileged children of fortune, but of man in general, the great mass of mankind. Science and politics have since developed along these lines, and their progress in this direction continues. It is not to be wondered at that I can join in without difficulty or effort.

I therefore feel that the solution of the riddle as to why some old men are able to keep in harmony with the changes of the times is to be sought in the fact that they foresaw and desired these changes during their youth and maturer years. They represent nothing new to their way of thought and of feeling, nothing that would require them to renounce their accustomed ideas, for the changes only confirm these. Such old men have not to struggle with the ultra-conservative tendencies of age, nor to deny old and accustomed ideas, before welcoming change. In contrast to them, old men who were satisfied with the conditions of bygone days and wish to preserve them will find it difficult in their old age to take on a new mentality. They will become the type of old man whom every change annoys, and it is probable that this type is in the majority.

Is the harmony between an active old age of the kind I have attempted to describe, and the mind of the younger generation, complete? Certainly, it is not. Such harmony depends upon the nature of progress and its objects. Age often grasps these objects better and more completely than youth, because it pursues them with a mature conviction, and not in the first flush of exuberant enthusiasm. For this reason, it is more able to criticise dispassionately and to set due limits, but it often lacks understanding of the younger generation's methods and ways of expression. The young are travelling along other roads to the same goal. Arguments which would be decisive for old age make no impression on younger minds, and vice versa. This applies equally to philosophical research, to the history of art, and to political endeavour. I do not say that in these differences of style youth is always right, and that every novelty represents a step forward, a definite enrichment of mankind's intellectual treasure. Much that is new is not progress, but a sign of decadence or a temporary delusion of the kind which always comes into being during periods of transition. Once a new style exists, however, neither age nor youth is competent to judge its merits, because both are interested parties, and only the future can decide.

This nuance dividing the older generation from the young who think like them is one of the reasons which have led me to declare already that the part best suited to age in active life is much more that of counsellor and critic than direct participant.

Such participation is not the forte of age. One often hears old age taxed with a lack of initiative and decision, and it is difficult for me to say how far this reproach is justified. An analogy with the failure of the muscles suggests itself, and leads one to presume a similar weakening in the power of the will. However, if this power has to be exercised at all by an old man, he often shows the greater endurance. It remains true, even so, that the keenness of decision in an old man is not equal to the keenness of thought which he may retain under favourable circumstances. If we compare the different ages of man while on this subject, we are inclined to say that desire is predominant in youth. The young have desires here, there, and everywhere, while they have comparatively little reflection. At maturity a balance establishes itself between the two forces of thought and volition, only to be upset again when a great age is reached, to the disadvantage of the will. Temperamentally, the old man does not desire, for, before desiring, he must awaken in himself the will to desire. Yet does this not agree with his sphere of activity in general? Is a man called upon to force his will on future generations, when in all probability he will no longer be alive to see the consequences of his desire? Apart from exceptional cases, this is not the true calling of old age. The wisdom which is stored up in it must, in most cases, find its way into younger intellects, if it would express itself in action. That is the normal course of things.

And here I will conclude, for I ought now to discuss an aspect of old age which cuts most deeply into the inward life, but which I could not attempt with the necessary thoroughness in this unpretentious essay. I refer to the contrast between one's feeling of intense, and often fruitful, vitality and the certainty of an approaching end. Does not a dark shadow fall here across the cheerful picture which I have drawn of a lively old age? Can this fullness of life resist the keen realisation of mortality? It is a serious question to which every old man must find an answer. Mine is that of the believing Christian for whom the end signifies a new beginning, and the darkness of death a transition to everlasting light. This conviction imparts to the soul a profound peace which allows it also to enjoy everything good and beautiful that age still offers, and, at the same time, to continue labouring cheerfully and without interruption at one's task, until the hour in which God Himself shall say: "Enough, my son!"